THE GIFT *of* WILL

M A R I E P A L M E R

with Lisa Cerasoli

STORY MERCHANT BOOKS
LOS ANGELES • 2018

The Gift *of* Will

ISBN-13: 978-1-7323411-9-7

Story Merchant Books
400 S. Burnside Avenue, #11B
Los Angeles, CA 90036
www.storymerchantbooks.com

www.529books.com
Interior Design: Lauren Michelle
Cover: Claire Moore

To Michael,

May your soul rest in peace on the other side.

———————

"There is no fear in love, perfect love casts out fear. Fear has torment. Those who fear are not made perfect in love."

I John 4:18

INTRODUCTION

I WAS BORN IN 1974. My brother was born in 1975, and my sister came into the world in 1977. We were born into an organization called the Children of God. We were second-generation disciples, as our parents were both followers. Spawned from the desires of one man, David Brant Berg created this community, separate from the mainstream, so he could live out a personal utopia that could generally be described as a hippie Jesus movement. Berg was a charismatic man with a magnetic personality. He called himself Moses David, which is how we referred to him, as well. Berg founded this group in 1969. My mother and father joined together around 1972.

About six years into our journey, after my younger sister was born, my mother decided to leave the organization. My father wanted to stay, so he kept my brother and me—we were three and two at the time—and my mother left with my sister, who was nine months.

It wasn't until twelve years later that my brother and I were able to escape and reunite with our mother.

• • •

Before I tell this story, there are a couple things that are important for you to know. First and foremost, this is my story. Most of the experiences in the cult environment in which I was raised happened twenty-eight-plus years ago. As much as you will hear about the pain, confusion, and isolation, it's important for me to state that I've also been assisted and even saved by various individuals and organizations over the years.

I do not describe my personal faith as that of a Christian, but I still believe there are organizations out there doing good things for others in the name of their faith and beliefs. I still support some of these organizations.

I write about some experiences involving my father and mother, and some of the details may seem petrifying. But, I now have a wonderful, though at times distant, relationship with both parents. Things are as good as they can be, thanks to my divergent thinking and capacity for forgiveness.

I wish no ill will or harm to any of the people I mention in this book. I wish no ill will to any separatist organization or cult. There are well-meaning people in every kind of community doing their best to help themselves, their families, and the world around them. I also understand that the cult provided a personal sanctuary for my parents at that juncture in their lives.

For me (and others like me), being a member of the cult wasn't a choice, but my destiny. Still, my views may not reflect the views, feelings, memories, or experiences of other second-generation adults who were also born into the organization.

My perspective in the telling of my story is geared toward empowering others to share their truth, whether or not they've been in a cult. As my reader, maybe you've had similar experiences in related or unrelated organizations. Or maybe you're reading purely out of curiosity because of the themes and motifs in this book. I want to tell my truth, and I hope in doing so that people who provoke these kinds of things get a good wake-up call. It's one thing to be born to loving parents that help you navigate through the beauty and ugliness of life. It is quite the opposite to have your soul, spirit, heart, mind, emotions, behaviors, consciousness, and rights of choice manipulated from birth without rational or compassionate guidance. To survive this sort of circumstance you have to die either literally or figuratively. That's the only way to find freedom, because to live within the walls of something you neither understand nor believe in is death itself. Exploitation and brainwashing—the basis of my upbringing—is not advocating for children's rights. Children have rights, too, and this book is my way of speaking out. I don't want anyone else to experience what I did. It's enough.

Most importantly, my story is about forgiveness. Proverbs 25:22 says, "By forgiving them, we reap coals of fire upon their heads." I forgive them without fear of retaliation, shame, blame, or guilt. Letting go and developing my relationship with the Divine has allowed me to exercise my human rights to free will, self-actualization, and self-expression.

In the cult, we were never taught to love ourselves or to put ourselves, our personal needs, or wants first. Self-love meant we were mocking Christ. We were supposed to deny ourselves in order to take up our cross. This book is me burning the Children of God cross I have carried all my life.

• • •

As an adult, I listen to a lot of music in my free-time. One band I'm drawn to is Tool. I like their thunder-and-lightning rhythms, and their overall sound. Years after college, in 2016, I was listening to them on Pandora, and decided to buy an album. I searched YouTube and happened on a tribute song that lead singer Maynard James

Keenan wrote for his mother, Judith Marie Keenan: "Wings for Marie." I thought, how ironic that someone would write a song for me. (Trust me, I am not that delusional. I am laughing right now.) I remember listening to it with a glass of wine and weeping like a baby, playing it over and over, just crying my eyes out at its beauty.

In this song, a son encourages his mother, who has passed on to the afterlife, to finally find the courage to stick up for herself. He's angry at the Divine Universe for allowing his mother to be so self-sacrificial to her own detriment while she was alive, and he's worried she won't get her "wings" if she doesn't find her own voice and ask for them. He tells her to be bold now, to rise with fury, to shake her fists at the gates of heaven (or hell) and demand what was hers to begin with: "Give me my wings!"

I remember thinking, as I often do, about self-love and what that means to me. And I thought about what it must mean to Maynard James Keenan, too. He wrote a song demanding that his mother find her courage, her love of self, so she can be at peace. If Judith can get her wings, why can't I get my wings, too?

Greek mythology speaks about the phoenix—a bird that is cyclically regenerated or reborn. According to the myth, the phoenix dies in a show of flame and combustion only to arise anew from the ashes of its predecessor.

Writing this book has helped me recognize that part of me has died—the part that was ignorant and unworthy of love or attention. What has risen is the beautiful animal-spirit being that I am now—conscious of myself, rising into awareness, understanding my own identity, my soul's desires, and my will to achieve.

This book is my phoenix rising from the ashes of defeat to become a dragon with rainbow wings. My inner dragon is strong, fierce, independent, and breathes the fire of creativity, life, and love.

My rainbow wings symbolize my tolerance for divergence in the world and in all sentient beings. We are all unique souls and should be respected for our individuality and for the gifts the Divine has given us. This book is my destiny; it is my rebirth; it is my revolt against all forms of child enslavement; it is my commentary on forgiveness; it is my contribution to humanity.

This book is my gift of will.

THE GIFT *of* WILL

AXON PRUNING is the process of synapse elimination in the brain. It starts near the time of birth and is completed by sexual maturation in humans and other select mammals. Pruning deactivates cells in the brain that are not being used. In concurrence with pruning, a process called APOPTOSIS can occur—the self-destruction of deactivated cells to prevent uncontrolled cell growth. The choice of which cells to deactivate and destroy is influenced by environmental factors and profoundly effects cognitive and emotional development into and throughout adulthood.[1]

---

[1] *Online Resource Dictionary*

Chapter

1

THE HUMAN BRAIN IS A platform for learning. When a baby is born, the calligraphy of life is sketched upon its mind, but the colors on the picture have yet to be filled in. Everything is new and fresh, simple, like a rudimentary drawing. A newborn baby doesn't have any conscious idea how to make connections; regardless, they will be formed from the beginning. The connections that aren't formed, will remain dormant for lack of use. (Perhaps a subconscious desire for certain connections may be there, but the actuality of it remains latent for lack of use.) The conscious brain or "everyday use" brain will then discard them, allowing the cells remaining to have room to evolve and adapt to the environment around them.

When a child is conditioned, he or she will perform according to the programs received through life experiences—sensations, emotions, and relations, interpersonal and interdependent. Babies cannot live by any other truth than the foundations that supports them; their lives and relations are dependent on the world that constructs their reality from the cradle on.

Upon maturation, the adult will have more control. But, if certain awareness isn't achieved, that person will fall into the same patterns by which they were conditioned in the first experiences of life.

This is part of the evolutionary process that makes us human beings. There is a sense of duality in the process of our evolution. We understand ourselves, others, and the world around us through the lenses of ideas, and projections that form concepts we label as good and evil, right and wrong, black and white, or, sometimes, in shades of gray. But, when the connections between reality, emotion, and spirituality are blurred and manipulated, the result will be a conglomeration of projections that are narrow. Brainwashing creates a small view of reality, one that fits into a box designed for the purpose of promulgating a singular cause. There is no space in that box for new ideas. And, life goes on, until evolution kicks in, which brings about a recognition of this new reality as skewed, which arouses a survival instinct.

A person's instinct to survive is the ultimate dominating factor in all life decisions big and small—unless (this is very crucial) that person loses all desire to live. In this case, they will go against their natural instincts to survive. This is what we call being suicidal, homicidal, or in a religious context it might be called allowing the self to die.

These types of individuals are vulnerable to the domination of others. This can be amended by finding a sense of uniqueness or identity, in spite of the projections imposed upon them. But, this shift requires an immense amount of strength in the form of self-love, self-respect, self-will, and a sincere desire to live for something bigger—a purpose.

The experiences we have as children, from birth to age six, are some of the most influential. They mold and shape who we are and determine who we will become as teenagers and, subsequently, as adults. Depending on what those experiences are, we might become confident and comfortable in our own skin, or, we might learn that the world is a terrifying place. If we don't get paradigms like the latter fixed, and quickly, we remain trapped inside them, paralyzed by patterns that are destructive to ourselves and others.

In 2005, sixteen years after leaving the Children of God, I took a science class where I learned about apoptosis and synaptic pruning, the brain's deactivation and shedding process. Years later, in 2016, I did a training course so that I could teach at a prison that housed youth, ages twelve to twenty-five. In that training, the instructors mentioned synaptic pruning and apoptosis. It was such a weird coincidence to have these terms applied to children that were a product of the prison system because I had felt for years that these terms applied to me.

I know those words sound fancy, but their processes are simple. Our brains are filled with connections, which give us an aptitude for multiple abilities. That is why, for example, if you want to teach your children to speak multiple languages, you should teach them when they are very young, even while they are learning their primary language, before the age of six.

Children are also better at learning different instruments, etc., when they are young, because the brain is open, it's a sponge, it's waiting to be activated, and apoptosis and synaptic pruning are on standby, so-to-speak, waiting in the wings to dictate what this child's brain uses, and then deactivating or laying parts dormant that it isn't using.

Think of aboriginals who are hunters and gatherers. Their lives depend on their sense of smell and their ability to hear the animals they track and hunt in the wild. This is their means for survival. These connections in their brains have been nurtured and developed.

If you stick a city girl like me into the world of an aboriginal and ask me to use my sense of smell and sound to track a deer in the forest, I couldn't do it, even if my survival depended on it. In my brain, those connections haven't been developed and are not actively being used. They died long ago through apoptosis. (Note: It's possible, but rare, in real-life, emergency situations that "dormant" survival techniques can be reawakened.)

I like to relate this to the animal self, because there is an emotion all humans and animals experience that is relevant to this discussion: fear. If a child learns that fear is a natural part of life, then that child will learn to expect fear. This emotion, this connection—fear equals life—is developed like a second language, or an acute sense of smell.

When I was a child, my father used a strong hand; he was a perpetual spanker, and so was his father, and likely his grandfather. My father was born in the era when spanking was considered a healthy and normal form of discipline, and then he joined a cult that encouraged the same tactics. It was a biblical ideology to spank children, utilizing fear to make them behave.

There is a scripture in the Bible from Proverbs 13:24 that we paraphrase nowadays: "Spare the rod, spoil the child." That phrase was used not only by biblical believers, but also by many parents as an appropriate justification for using violence in order to ensure obedience from their children.

Whenever I would do something naughty, like run in the house or lie, my father would spank me. The same went for my brother. Of course, since I was a girl, he went easier on me.

I recall a specific incident when I was no more than five or six. I cannot for the life of me remember what I had done, but my father had me sit in the closet for what seemed like hours, praying to Jesus for forgiveness. Eventually, he decided to rescue me from the closet to face a worse punishment, which was my spanking. I remember being terrified. I prayed diligently and desperately to his Lord to please come into my heart and forgive me for my sins. I wanted so badly to be rescued from the inevitable spanking.

I know my father was trying to instruct me to be righteous and holy, just as his father and, subsequently, Moses David was instructing him. He wanted me to understand right from wrong. Regardless, what these methods taught me was that fear was a motivator for good behavior.

I lived in perpetual fear with the Children of God. I wanted to prevent myself from slipping up again, from being naughty and ending up with a similar ritual over and over. And, I did try, hard, to be perfect, to go unnoticed. I worked like crazy to be invisible when I was a young girl.

During my life, anger and terror were the connections I was developing in my brain. Living in fear was the way to exist. This was learned behavior. To steer clear of admonishment—in the shape of being locked in a dark closet for hours—I learned to modify my behavior accordingly, to the point where I began to effectively read my father's mind. I would do as I knew he wished to eliminate pain and embarrassment from my world. As such, my brain was developing a sense of stimulus/response.

In the 1890s, Russian physiologist Ivan Pavlov conducted one of the most prominent experiments on conditioning in history. As the majority of you know, it consisted of a dog, food, and a bell. The master would ring the bell, and food was presented to the dog. The dog would salivate upon seeing it. Soon, all the master had to do was ring the bell, and, even when there was no food, the dog would salivate. It had been classically conditioned to respond that way. Pavlov tried this with various dogs of different breeds and sexes and they all responded in the same way.

When I was young while all my patterns were being formed, I was also being conditioned to behave a certain way, as every child is. I became so accustomed to the spanking part of my punishments that, at some point, something triggered, and whenever my father would give me a look, I would behave as such to avoid the punishment.

To be clear, two scientific paradigms were being created. One, the neurons in my brain were forming patterns of learning: to relate to my environment. Two, conditioning was occurring: how to respond to outside stimuli.

As I got older, being a second-generation disciple, life got more intense. After being conditioned to act a specific way—invisible—I graduated to being conditioned to believe as the cult believed. Without question. Before long, the synapses in my young brain were solidified. Connections intended to cultivate joy, trust, and confidence in myself and others had been severed for lack of use.

• • •

I remember parts of my childhood vividly. My earliest memory is of sitting in a high chair with a sippy cup. (This was back when my father and mother were still together.) I recall my parents arguing about something. It upset me greatly. I threw my sippy cup to the floor in protest.

Their anger then shifted to me. The whole room turned a shade of red. I imagine it was my compulsive crying and screaming that upset them. I remember the look on my father's face—the one I would grow to respond to like Pavlov's dog. He came over to the high chair to ensure my tantrum stopped....

I aim to paint a picture of my memories. They appear to me as if they happened yesterday. Sometimes they feel as if they're in real time, occurring in some parallel universe. It's like I'm a dragonfly on the wall, watching another human being as she navigates through life.

The impressions made on my mind when I was a young child were emphatically real and live with me today as my eyes, heart, bones, and limbs do. I don't believe I'm the only adult that can recollect vivid, dreamlike memories of experiences they had when they were children. But, I do believe mine are more electric and detailed than the average person's due to the unfortunate synaptic connections that were both fused and severed in my brain early on.

Since my brain was wired to think a certain way to avoid pain, I was conditioned to be afraid of displeasing my father, which then translated into any authority. This has been my truth since that memory of throwing my sippy cup in the high chair. My self-identity and will were manipulated through fear to adhere to certain principles and behaviors. Yet, my true identity (my true self, my unique soul) was buried somewhere inside, dying to get out and just "be."

But, I never got the chance to grow or develop in a healthy, safe environment. I was being conditioned to become a product of what my father and the Children of God wanted, with the stratagem being the annihilation of all sense of self.

And they did this in the name of God.

Chapter

2

DURING THE EARLY 1970s, THERE was a sincere longing for something more. Many young people were disillusioned with everything that had happened the decade before, including drafts for the war in Vietnam, too much access to drugs, and poverty and homelessness that were becoming mainstream due to young Americans dropping out of school and generally rebelling against these myriad causes and more.

Both my parents had experienced some kind of relief and hope from joining an organization that seemed to want to preserve and develop their ideals, all the while taking care of them. As most people, I can look back on my child rearing and view some of it as beneficial to my development as an adult. But, the majority of what I was taught—the cult's philosophy—I refer to as brainwashing.

There were a lot of people in this group that loved their faith very much and lived in that truth. They were radical. They were revolutionary. They were trying to find a way to strip themselves of selfish desires, in order to end personal misery and find purpose in life.

I understand the passionate desire that drives human beings to find other human beings that feel the same way they do. By nature, we strive for connection. Finding people that think the way "we think" gives us a sense of stability, security, a sense of belonging, a feeling of "everything is going to be okay."

I learned in college that this is called groupthink.

Usually, a charismatic leader reassures the flock that as long as they follow a certain groupthink thought process, everything will work out. This is what is known as the law of attraction and the power of intention. Paradigm shift philosophers like Abraham and Esther Hicks, authors of *The Secret*, among others, write extensively on this *like attracts like* pattern. Whatever our hearts believe will materialize, because, even if we don't talk about it, our desire to be *this way* or *that way* is expressed energetically. This means any given population or group naturally attracts other like-minded souls to go on said journey with them. And this is done without much effort; again, it's about energy. So, when the leader of these types of organizations, groups, cults, gangs, clubs, institutions, etc., gains control and power over their "flock" of like-minded individuals, they gain the power to shift the collective way of thinking, which then creates action.

In the cases of leaders like Gandhi, Martin Luther King, Nelson Mandela, and such, positive humanitarian change occurs in the world because of their message and influence, elevating consciousness, and instigating humanitarian actions and good will toward others. But this control can be dark, too. In the case of Moses David, he used his power to instill fear, guilt, and shame to influence and control weaker but like-minded individuals. Fear helps ensure loyalty to a cause or organization, and shame and guilt dictate behavior: To be subservient. To be violent. To protest. To be mute. To allow emotional and/or physical abuse to happen to others. To drink poison. To become child molesters. To become willing victims of molestation and sexual assault. To even do things that, in other circumstances, those individuals might never do. To rape, steal, murder, and even die for "the cause."

Before my father joined, he was a hippie. He was into drugs and bell bottoms. He had an afro that would have made Diana Ross jealous. He was introduced to this cult by my mom's brother, who, at the time, thought it was far out. They believed in free love—in burning bras and being generally free from the confines and rules of the traditional world. They wanted to get back down to the basics of life.

This movement, spearheaded by David Brant Berg (a.k.a. Moses David, as mentioned) was based on stories from the Bible. He had a religious upbringing and had broken free from traditional Christian "restraints." Moses David believed the laws of man were useless, and the rules that civilization lived by were falling apart. He believed God's only law was love, and that he was chosen to be a prophet of the End Times, as predicted in the biblical Book of Revelations. Moses David was here to set the captives free, and to be a witness to the End of the World and the ushering in of a heaven on earth.

He essentially found a handful of lost kids and persuaded them to follow him. Together, with him at the helm, they marched in sync to a hippie Jesus tune, while Moses David grew his marching band, his army, creating an organization that led hundreds, and eventually thousands, of hippies and others of the like to revolutionize a new world and leave the materialistic one, from which they were raised, behind.

These people were longing for something that only they could understand, define, and live by. Much like St. Francis of Assisi, they believed in shedding the material for the spiritual. They wanted to live like beggars, like Jesus and his disciples.

This freedom included commune-style living. Even though there were couples, like my parents, Moses David advocated the notion of the collective over the couple. His one-love philosophy was ripped directly from a biblical scripture: "For in the resurrection they neither marry, nor are given in marriage, but are as the angels of God in Heaven" (Matthew 22:30).

The best way to describe what Moses David cultivated in modern-day terms is to say he was creating a community of swingers, where age and sex had no bearing on behavior. Couples could share their bodies in the act of physical love with others outside their partnership. And they were encouraged to. But, no form of contraception was allowed. The flock was told to trust the Lord, which meant copulating often resulted in pregnancy. You procreate—period. In record time, Moses David had created a new army of Children of God disciples—the second generation.

When I turned the age of three, around 1977, the free love got to be a little too much for my mother. She was more concerned about raising the three kids she'd had with our father inside the walls of the organization than about procreating with other men in the group. She did not want to share her body in any kind of ritual of unselfish sacrifice, affection, or love. And my guess is she didn't want any more children, at least not while she was living as a beggar under someone else's ruling.

Often, people who were not willing to share their bodies in the name of love were considered selfish and not "in the Spirit." Remember, we were taught that loving ourselves first was an abomination. Putting ourselves first—including our desires, wants, needs, attractions, or anything natural—was neglecting the path to this form of holiness.

All these conceptualizations of reality were justified by scriptures in the Bible. Moses David had one for this law, too. The Bible talks about the natural man being a shameful, weak thing. We should surrender the natural desires or what the natural being wants and follow more spiritual things.

Ephesians 4:22–24 says, "[22]You were taught, with regard to your former way of life, to put off your old self, which is being corrupted by its deceitful desires; [23]to be made new in the attitude of your minds; [24]and to put on the new self, created to be like God in true righteousness and holiness."

This was interpreted to mean that our natural attractions or desires were not necessarily aligned with the spiritual.

Twisted into a communal viewpoint, it promoted self-sacrifice on behalf of those followers that were not as desirable or without mates. In other words, even though you may not have been attracted to a follower, if they expressed their desire toward you, you were expected to submit. Meeting the sexual needs of every C.O.G. cult member was paramount regardless of age or gender.

It wouldn't be until 1987–88, around the time I was hitting puberty, I started to recognize this philosophy. As a result, a profound, unimaginable fear took root inside me.

Chapter

3

A CHILD DOESN'T HAVE THE luxury of choosing their parents. Some religions believe we choose that destiny from the other side, coming from a place where God keeps souls—the Hall of Souls. Some believe we are born into this or that familial scenario via karma. Proving my brother or I deserved to be born into cult life, or chose it, is impossible and futile.

Because my dad's heart was in the organization, my parents ended up splitting in 1977. My mom was so desperate to get out, to move on, to find some stability and security in her own personal identity, she made the ultimate sacrifice to achieve that—she left my brother and me with my father, took our new sister, and got the hell out.

On the heels of my mom's departure, my dad found himself another woman. It was love at first sight. She came from a Jewish family outside the cult. He worked diligently to convert her to the Jesus movement, and, as they fell in love, she decided to join my father on his mission. Once they were officially together, she followed him like a puppy.

We eventually ended up in Europe as a new family: my father, his new girlfriend, my brother, and me. We traveled in various makes and models of RV and trailers. We used to sing on the streets about God and the message my father preached. We were gypsy hippies, and our street productions allowed us the opportunity to support ourselves.

It was right before my sixth birthday—we had been in Europe about a year—when I saw the most amazing baby doll in the window of a store. I remember holding my father's hand and slowing our pace as we walked past it. I longed for it with fierce and hopeful eyes and begged my father to buy it.

On my birthday, he walked into our trailer with a big smile, bringing me a gift. Lo and behold it was that baby dolly. I think my dad might still have a picture of me smiling and holding it. He loved to take pictures. He also got my brother some roller skates. I remember my brother hobbling along as he tried to figure out how to use them. It was the happiest day of my life.

You might think this is silly, but as an adult, I found another baby dolly that reminded me of the only one I'd ever owned as a little girl. I purchased it. She still resides in my bedroom, propped on a dresser, big-eyed with her head cocked, a reminder that I did have happy days as a child.

After our year-long European adventure of traveling, singing, preaching, and begging, we had to fly back to America. There's a verse in the Bible that talks about forsaking all for God—in other words, ditching your material belongings to find holiness and spirituality. Mathew 19:29 says, "And everyone who has left houses or brothers or sisters or father or mother or wife or children or fields for my sake will receive a hundred times as much and will inherit eternal life."

My brother and I were forced to give up the dolly and roller skates. For two children who didn't have anything, it was devastating.

I understand now that my father was doing what he believed was right. He felt the world was raising kids all wrong, just as he had been raised before he joined the organization—to love toys and games, to crave fun, freedom, candy, gifts, laughter, and the list goes on. The world was a trap that would ensnare anyone. He wanted to be free from it. His devotion was pure-hearted to the core. He desired to step into the light. Nothing and no one would stop him from achieving his goal, especially not any children he fathered. We were his chance to get it right. If he could get a five- and six-year-old to renounce all material belongings, including toys, that was the definition of spiritual enlightenment. A ticket into heaven for certain.

• • •

Since biblical indoctrination was so essential to our C.O.G. training, most of the movies we watched were religious. We did watch some others; Moses David seemed to have an infatuation with old musicals and actors like Gene Kelly and Fred Astaire. But, otherwise, we watched movies with Charlton Heston in them, and other films that illustrated Christian martyrs dying for their faith.

The movie we watched more than any other was *Jesus of Nazareth*—a three-volume series that depicted the life of Jesus, including his gruesome death. I don't remember the exact number of times we watched that movie, but over the course of my fourteen years in the C.O.G., I would guess at least a hundred.

I can't even begin to describe the effects the crucifixion scene had on my young, impressionable mind. I remember feeling terrified of a god that would allow something like that to happen to his own son. *That was his will? And, all of humanity was to blame for it including me, innocent as I was?* The film, which seemed to be on permanent repeat at our community center, did not alleviate or numb me to this fear, as is sometimes the result of conditioning. It reaffirmed it.

The guilt I felt was overwhelming. We were taught that even though we did not physically kill Jesus, humanity was stained with the guilt of sin, and because of that sinful nature, we were all responsible for his death. The only way to be redeemed was to accept his blood sacrifice as penance. Not only did I feel personally responsible for the death of God's son, but a sick thought was birthed in my mind as a direct result of seeing this film over and over and over—one that whispered I was evil.

How cruel to be forced to believe that any divine creator would put a tree in a garden to tempt humanity, and then punish his people for thousands of years with the final verdict: sinful and fallen. Then, only with blood, blood, and more blood, was there a chance at redemption. Regardless, history would have to continue to fight the stain of sin until the end of time. Then, somehow through death, we would all be redeemed—if we believed hard enough. The perpetual struggle from birth to death was inevitable. This was the C.O.G. philosophy.

Even from a very early age, I could not understand the concept of my creator or creators being so naïve or punitive that they would construct a reality in which, they, being all-knowing, would place a temptation so powerful in our midst. Wouldn't an all-knowing creator know he'd set us up for failure, a lose-lose situation? If we chose to do the inevitable, which was eat of the forbidden fruit, we would be punished for life with the promise of death. Living a sin-free life is impossible, particularly for children who live in the moment, who don't understand that natural wants are sinful. Desiring toys means worshipping false gods. Wanting candy is being glutinous. Laughter and self-love is mocking God. I was living with a ticking time bomb inside me. One false move and....

Chapter

4

THE BULK OF OUR CHILDREN'S stories were written by Moses David. There were volumes and volumes of them. Some were beautiful and interesting. All were aimed to simplify my feelings about my life. They made me feel like I was special because I was part of this organization. They made me feel loved, cared for, and nurtured as part of the collective—their intention was strong and effective.

As I was a second-generation Children of God disciple, I was chosen by God for a special mission, a purpose. They tried to exemplify a sort of innocence we all longed for, even in our stain of sin. The goal was to ensure us that since we were all fallen, we might as well embrace that as truth and do our best to love Jesus in spite of it. We were to trust that He would make all things well, even given our shame and incompetency.

The things I could not swallow were much darker. Moses David wrote so many volumes of books and letters that advocated self-berating, self-belittling, and pejorative conceptualizations of humanity. Who we were as human beings would never be enough. We were unworthy. We were filthy. We were dirty. We were stained. We were never going to be sinless on this earth. The price to pay for freedom was our souls, our wills, and our entire physical selves.

The use of fear as a motivator is ingrained in many cultures throughout the world. I can't remember a waking moment of my cult life where fear in some form was not used as a motivator. Right from the beginning, in the story of the Garden of Eden, God used fear by punishing and shaming all of humanity—past, present, and future—for the Fall of Man. God allowed the tree of the knowledge of good and evil to exist in the Garden of Eden. We were too curious, too seduced to resist, and we have paid dearly for that sin.

Straying from the cult or being a divergent thinker was considered one of the bigger sins, worthy of punishment. Never mind that it was a violation of human rights; it was a violation of the cult's system, and this was something that was not done.

Moses David had the artists among us depict the themes of his letters to the members of his organization with vibrant imagery.

On the front cover of a letter called "The Helmet," there was a picture of a man with a knight's helmet on his head. Above it, someone was hammering a nail into his skull. This idea came from one of the many dreams of Moses David.

The Mo Letter (as each was designated) was all about how we needed to drive the word of God into our heads like an iron hammer drives a nail through a metal helmet into a human skull. The idea was that we needed to get God's Word, and get it good, to the point of pain and death, if necessary.

Now that I can understand the depth of what this picture represented to my childhood, I'm outraged. This image—a nail being driven through a helmet into a human skull—symbolizes everything I was raised to believe. When I first read this Mo Letter and saw the image of this scared, hunched-over man in a knight's helmet, I remembered thinking how typical it was, typical as in "normal."

Was it? Typical? Did other children from regular families see illustrations of soldiers with nails being drilled into their heads? The underlying message was that we were too thickheaded to understand God's Word, and needed a nail driven through our skulls to combat our ignorance. Were there tactics such as this out in the "real world," the one my father was protecting us from? Were those tactics in the vain of the Mo Letters?

As children, we never discussed any of our feelings about these Mo Letters with each other. We knew that was taboo. So, I worked to suppress my feelings, to suck it up and deal with my everyday reality.

When it was time for our indoctrination, which happened over the course of many years leading up to puberty, we would read different Mo Letters. Then, we'd have to write about our reactions to what we'd read. I always knew exactly what to say to please my father. My reactions were never genuine. I just wrote what I knew they wanted us to think. I was ensuring my safety and staying in my father's good graces. I didn't want to be spanked, as I was too old for that. I didn't want to be shoved into a closet for hours on bent knees praying. But, above all, I didn't want to break. I didn't know what would happen should that bomb that was living inside me detonate. So, yes, I had decided I'd best play the game, as freedom wasn't within my reach.

In my early teens, when these true feelings became hard to hide, I still could not fully comprehend them. It wasn't until recently, as an adult, that I have been able to unearth exactly what was happening to me back then. I remember knowing there was something wrong with my environment, but I was too young, too weak, and too brainwashed to take my marching band of one and fight against a group of thousands. By this point, the Children of God was a living, breathing, worldwide organization.

Today, as a free-thinking woman, I cringe and sometimes cry when I recall the fear tactics that were used to keep me in line. But I understand that my inability to cry out was about survival more than anything.

There was another Mo Letter called "Backsliders Beware." The picture on the front cover was of a naked man going down a slide backwards—ass first. His neck was twisted all the way around and he had the most petrified facial expression. At the bottom of the slide there was fire. He was going to hell. The idea was that if we left the organization, we were doomed to hellfire. The picture on the front spoke a thousand words; reading the letter wasn't even necessary. But trust me; we all read it, and his letters were typically very, very long.

There were many other illustrations sketched for the Mo Letters. Many depicted the use of fear tactics. One of them was created in the image of one of our divergent disciples. Her name was Deborah. She came into our domain when I was reaching my early teens. She was astonishingly beautiful. Moses David tried to seduce her and turn her into one of his lovers. He wanted to get her to follow the principles of the organization. He even wanted her to lead the organization with him. She resisted. In the end, she defied his authority and left. She was depicted as a gorgeous goddess on the front page of one letter after that. She was a queen with saddened eyes. The letter was about how she had so much potential to be not only his queen but a queen for the organization, except her heart was not pure enough. She had too much pride, rendering her unworthy of the crown.

There was another Mo Letter called "Are You Deaf?" The picture on the front was of a young boy riding his bicycle on the street next to a semi-truck. The truck was honking. It was clear from the carefree look on the boy's face that he was deaf to the horn, the danger of the semi-truck, oblivious of everything.

The letter was asking us: *Are you so deaf you can't hear God speaking to you? Are you so deaf that your human nature would block the sound and sight of danger all around you?* We were about to be run over by a semi-truck. That was the message.

Mo used fear to convince us we were handicapped, deaf fools. We were disabled people who couldn't hear God speak. And the Mo Letters always depicted a godhead that found us loathsome fools, as Mo's God was a vengeful one, one that wanted retribution for our innate brokenness. The irony, ultimately, was that we were taught God was love, and love was the only law. But, the undercurrent that existed, the subliminal message was that we were merely fallen, lost children, dumb sheep, and doomed to be co-dependent on the word of God through the Prophet Mo. If you break a person down enough they're bound to seek and accept love any way they can get it.

And that was Moses David's plan.

There was another Mo Letter called "Teen Terrors." It was about teenagers that were born into this organization but did not comply with the rules, regulations, and ideas of the group—they were considered "terrors." A terror was anyone who spoke out. A terror was anyone who decided that something in our mainstream cult was wrong. A terror was anyone who did not yield and obey without question. We were terrors because we were a threat to conformity. We asked *why* questions, and there was no room for such things. I was a terror in my heart for years, living with that guilt before finding the courage to live my truth.

According to the Children of God leaders, our group was the epitome of right. We were "It." Anything that was not It was basically of the world, which was of the Devil. We terrors were doomed to face eternal damnation in the fires of hell or in the deceitful grasp of the world, which was owned and ruled by the Devil, which was synonymous with hell.

The pain and shame and worthlessness that my brother and I experienced defined us when we left, becoming self-fulfilling prophecies. We were derivative of the abuse and severe neglect at the hands of the Children of God cult. We rebelled against the organization's ability to keep us under their thumb, quiet and subservient. We made it out alive but didn't know how to adapt once we entered the real world.

In order to emphasize the importance of submitting to Mo, as well as the group psychology, philosophy, dogma, and leadership, there were many letters written about yielding to the authority of the group. We had to "yes, ma'am" and "yes, sir" every question. No arguing. No divergent opinions. No will of our own.

There was this Mo Letter called "Are You Willing to Sign a Blank Sheet of Paper?" It was about how if we wanted to serve God, then we would need to sign a blank sheet of paper. God—or the C.O.G. leaders—would write our lives on the sheet, and we would just accept it. The idea was that Mo and various leaders would write what they wanted us to be, think, or do. We were asked to sign the sheet of paper that symbolized giving our lives to whatever was written. We must do whatever God told us to, as interpreted by Mo and the leadership without question or negation. We would give up our will for the good of God and the group. This truth was under the guise of what was called "hearing from the Lord," as if God through Jesus was speaking to us directly. But, for me, there was no hearing from their Lord; there was only doing what I was told and obeying without question. My heart was already conflicted by their belief system, but no one ever gave me a choice to reject their ideologies or form opinions or ideas of my own. I would succumb to the groupthink or be considered an outsider. There was not another way.

Our brainwashing was also a sugar-coated pill; it wasn't all gun-held-to-the-temple fear tactics. Even though the message was harsh at times, there was always a gentle, nurturing, and loving alternative side. Some other Mo letters were soft and gentle. They were written to make us feel loved and cared for. They were letters about how God loved us, and how we were the End-time army of God fighting for truth. This was especially empowering because we were told that the world was going to end soon, and we would have a special place in heaven for sacrificing our wills and lives. We were told that Jesus would honor us in a special way, and that Mo would have a leadership role in heaven with us at his right side. If we did not surrender our will, then we were not worthy to be called good, godly, or righteous.

The one thing they did not seem to anticipate was that some of us would stand up and ask *why* questions, like children do. It was those questions that were so dangerous to the organization. The teens who asked *why*—the "terrors" as was the moniker—experienced ragged and cold intimidation tactics. I was a terror. I remember feeling like I was an illusion. My body and mind were theirs and I, alone, was not anything. That's when that feeling of heaviness, of not existing on the inside, began. I felt like I was drowning inside an enclosed vessel—a body—that didn't belong to me.

So much of my true self—the part of me that was yet undiscovered—was drowning in their indoctrination. My true self was stifled.

We were told not to justify ourselves. Justifying our ideas, thoughts, or dissonance with anything we felt in our internal guidance system was wrong, was a direct violation of the subservient nature that was imposed upon us.

We were never to question authority.

We were never to speak our own point of view.

We were sheep and we needed to follow without question.

We were children, we had no voice.

I recall another Mo Letter: "School." On the front was a drawing of a very sexy girl. She had dark, sad eyes. She stood behind barbed wire with books in her hands. Behind her was a building, an abandoned school. This letter was about how the education of the world was of the Devil. Education would only teach us more lies. This was a typical exposition on why we should not leave to find ourselves, much less go to public school. We were homeschooled by our parents or others in the organization. I cannot remember learning any math or science. We definitely did not learn about history or social studies. That would open our minds to too much of the outside world, and that was taboo. Mostly, we were taught to read and write so we could be indoctrinated. We read Mo letters every day. We had group sessions in the morning, and then individual indoctrination during our quiet time—writing down our reactions and what we learned. And even though we lived in cities where we used the money we made by selling our literature and music to pay rent, utilities, etc., we never played with neighborhood children.

Moses David suffered from a self-inflicted controversy over the idea of sin itself. Although he believed that we were inevitably born into sin, he also believed that the idea of sex and sexuality was part of original innocence. He believed that before we ate the forbidden fruit, we were able to enjoy the pleasures of sexuality without sin.

He also believed the only law of God was love (his idea of love, anyway). I realize now that Moses David got off on all the control, and the sex. Maybe on a subconscious level, or maybe consciously, the Children of God was created to feed his inner desires.

There was a Mo Letter called "Homos." On the front cover was a picture of two naked men who looked like brothers. One was lying down, and the other one was on his knees. They were engaged in what the Bible calls sodomy. The letter was his own internal demons battling as to whether or not sodomy was allowed by biblical scripture. I don't think Mo was bi-sexual. He wrestled with the idea that if God's only law was love, then perhaps homosexuality was permissible. He would toy with scriptures in the Bible to speculate on many things—this was one of them.

Through these letters, Mo went through his own form of spiritual catharsis. All his followers were soaked in his inner battles. We became a part of his stories. We were part of the journey of Mo managing his demons and angels. We lived in his personal heaven and hell.

Some letters were about jealousy and how it was a vicious snake that would kill you in a heartbeat. This was primarily because we believed in sexual freedom. So, if a mate were to get jealous of another man or woman having sexual relations with another person outside their partnership, it was considered to be unspiritual (the jealous third party was considered unspiritual). That person had contempt for the meaning of the freedom of the revolution. In that freedom, we neither married, nor were given in marriage, but were like the angels. We were like the disciples, parting everything in common.

Regardless of the intentions of these letters, I always felt like I was being exposed to adulthood. Even as a young child, my mind questioned it, felt overwhelmed by it, felt uneasy to the point of being terrified. My innocence was polluted with these deep, dark, demonic stories. It was polluted and darkened by the light that Mo felt Jesus was, a light which he "represented." I never had a chance to connect with who I was and neither did my brother.

And so, the story of our lives were a culmination of the sentiments and stories of our leader. My father followed his every word like gospel. My brother and I were abandoned, left to fill ourselves with Mo David's indoctrination as we interpreted it with our young minds.

No one ever asked us how we felt, who we were, or what we wanted. No one seemed to care what our talents or skills were, or what our destiny might be. If our views and hopes and dreams were not in line with the indoctrination of the organization, they were useless. Like everything else of the world, they were borne of the Devil himself and unworthy of the greater crown and purpose.

Mo was our King. He was aligned with Jesus. God was his alibi. Who can do any wrong, when you have the Almighty as your alibi for all that you say and do? Who can argue with that? Mo admitted that he wasn't perfect, and that he was a sinner, too. But he was the End-time prophet. So, at the end of each day, it was his way or the highway. No will, no imagination, no ideas, no paths of our own. He owned us, and we were his. For better or worse.

Chapter

5

MY FIRST SEXUAL EXPERIENCE WAS when I was about eleven years old, around 1985. My father went out of town on an organizational business trip. He left my brother (ten at the time) and me in the care of another couple. The adult male and his wife took advantage of us with sexual experimentation. I believed my father knew nothing about this at the time. (That seems naïve to me now. How could he not know?) Our father, like many people in that organization, was truly in love with its mission and purpose and blind to anything beyond that.

At the time of the experimentation, I didn't think anything of being naked with this adult man, who was probably in his thirties.

I was too young and too brainwashed to feel violated. I didn't even understand what was happening. It felt fun and innocent at first, normal, a game. I only knew it was wrong when I mentioned talking about it afterward. Their reaction to the thought of my brother and me telling others was extreme. This is when guilt set in.

This is when a recognition of what had been done to us took affect inside my conscious mind, and it scared the innocence right out of my heart.

Years later, in 2016, in my training for teaching, I learned about sexual molestation. I learned that it's normal for the victim to fear hurting the victimizer—so she (or he) will keep quiet about the assault(s). The victim experiences mixed emotions. There are so many emotional layers at the surface in an abuse victim. There can be fear mixed with compassion (for their assaulter) mixed with pleasure (which is a mere physical response) mixed with anger. This hyper-stimulation of emotions can be so overwhelming, the only way to manage it is to shove it into a dark place—into the subconscious.

The thirty-something-year-old man that had sexual relations with me, a pre-pubescent girl, realized that I might tell. My emotions were clear. He threatened to tell my father I had misbehaved. He said that I might get a spanking if I told my father what had happened. I remember him putting a thermometer in my mouth. He told me that I was sick and I needed help. My brother experienced a similar thing with the man's wife. The fear was so intense. The shame was so great. I thought I would die. Even if I couldn't talk about it, in my subconscious, I knew I would never be the same again.

• • •

When I started to mature from a child to a young girl, I was honored by being sent to a teen camp. This happened two years later, the summer of 1987 or 1988. (It was a four-week spiritual "getaway.") For the well-behaved teenagers that were subservient to the mission and ministry of our purpose, it was our reward. During this camp, we went on a spiritual quest within our hearts and souls. The adults wanted to prepare us for the End Times, and for being a witness to our mission and purpose as missionaries.

When the camp ended, I was invited to live in a special home for teens in Peru—this happened around the end of 1988. I was almost fourteen. We were exposed to a lot of openness regarding sexual attitudes and behaviors. We were encouraged to share our bodies with other young boys in the home. After all, there is a biblical scripture that says to be in an open commune, you need to have all things in common, sell all possessions and goods, and attend to every man as they had need.

"And all that believed were together, and had all things common; and sold their possessions and goods, and parted them to all men, as every man had need" (Acts 2:44,45 KJV).

That meant if there was a boy that needed affection, it was our duty to share our bodies to fulfill that need.

The first day I arrived, I was shown my "room"—an area full of bunk beds, like summer camp. We were separated, the girls from the boys. I remember one night I was in the bottom bunk, another girl had the upper bunk. We were chatting after the lights were out. During our whisperings, she had placed her arm down the side of the bed. I reached mine out and our fingers touched. I remember feeling the sexual excitement of this young girl's hand intertwined with my own. We began to massage one another's arms. It was long after the rest of the girls had gone to bed.

She snuck down the stairs that connected her bunk to mine. She whispered in my ear that we should go into the closet. This particular closet was a walk-in that led to the girls' bathroom. We crept inside and laid down on the floor, then we began to kiss and massage each other.

The passion we felt was too great to bear. We took off our pajamas. We made love on the floor until we both climaxed, releasing so much pent-up sexual pressure. We could barely contain ourselves. Once we were satisfied, she placed her finger against my lips. She was older, and more in charge than I was. She wanted to make sure that I would keep silent. She motioned for me to put my pajamas back on and go to the bathroom, like I had to pee. She used her hands to signal that she would go back first and climb into her bunk. I could go later.

I followed her instruction.

The adrenaline that rushed through my veins was incomparable to anything I'd ever felt. At that moment of connection, I felt truly in love or at least in lust with this girl.

I woke up obsessing over her. I remember looking at the other girls, day after day. I wasn't as pretty as they were. I didn't really have a best friend as many of the girls did. I felt that I was stocky and awkward. All I could do for the life of me was blend in and nothing more. So when this girl found herself admiring me, it was like all of the energy in my body ignited. I was on fire. I craved her. I wanted more.

Later that next day, she and I were called into a meeting with some of the leadership. They confronted us, asking if we had been experimenting together. I told them no. I was petrified. *How in the world did they find out? Did they hear us? Did they see us?* It turned out my partner in crime had confessed that morning. I was mortified.

Even though this organization was very open about sexual experimentation, I still felt guilty and betrayed. The other girl smiled. The leadership thanked her for her honesty. They returned her loving smile, then shifted that smile to me. They let me know that I had nothing to hide. They said what we had done was okay and completely normal.

I left that meeting confused. I couldn't believe they didn't enact some kind of punishment or separate us from each other. We continued to play for a while longer. I noticed that it wasn't just us— other girls and boys were experimenting, too. We were all having sexual encounters of some sort or another at our teen home in Peru.

My hormones were out of control. I was told to have no self-will and to yield on request. The only thing I knew was that I had to do whatever was encouraged by other followers, young and old.

They instructed us that a suggestion was an order given in love: you did what you were told, without questioning authority. How many times had I heard that since birth? One thousand times? One million? I was a hot mess. I was extremely attracted to older men because of my first sexual experience. I was also attracted to the boys that already had partners, even at that young age. I understand now that this was because I imagined they had some kind of maturity, which indicated they could take responsibility if I were to get pregnant.

This all happened in my subconscious back then, though, and I had no one to talk to, and no one to help me. I recognized my fears and patterns of behavior, but there was no conscious awareness, not like I have now. All I knew was what I wanted. The answers as to why came much later.

As I mentioned, the C.O.G. didn't believe in birth control—we just had to trust the Lord. You can only imagine how terrified I was when I saw other girls pregnant by fifteen. Some of them had no partner or mate. They just saddled a baby and went about with the prescribed rituals and chores we had to do each day (the chores being anything from vacuuming to kitchen duties).

I was scared to death. I wanted out. That was when my self-will kicked in hard. Now, I look back and understand it was simple self-preservation. It was the natural effect of evolution, of Darwinism, of my inner self telling me that to survive this crazy experience without getting knocked up, I had to get out and get out fast.

I had no self-identity. I was never given the power to choose anything. I didn't know who I was outside the indoctrination. How in the universe could I make decisions about my body? Yet, it was starting to happen....

Chapter

6

Months Later

I HAD BEEN SHIPPED OFF on another spiritual mission in Peru. I remember one afternoon we were read a story about one of the young teens who had backslid (gone against the cult). She had "left her post and deserted her plow" (Luke 9:62). She left the organization, became a backslider, a wasteland. She used drugs. She ended up lost in the world. The "Beast" took her into its grasp. She was gone. According to the Bible, if a person deserts their plow, they are no longer worthy of the Kingdom of God. The purpose of this story was to scare the hell out of us teenagers, so we wouldn't leave. It worked. It scared me to death. And, so, I had been living in a state of constant panic since I'd turned twelve. I had to get out; yet, the thought of leaving was paralyzing. (Eventually, leaving would scare me less than the thought of getting pregnant did.)

To top it off, I'd always had vivid dreams of things that a child should never be dreaming about. I faced a certain level of maturity I was not ready for when I was born into the cult, and I think the lifestyle must have affected my dreamlife. So, around this time, right before things began to change drastically, I had a dream about my biological mother. She was coming up the hill to our teen home with a bunch of South American witches called Macumberos. Macumba is a religion in Brazil that uses sorcery and fetish rituals. Somehow, all the fear I was experiencing was building up in my psyche. I felt her coming for me. During my waking hours, I was terrified of everything and everyone and, now, at night, I was dreaming of my mother and sorcerers.

Right before I left the teen home, something happened that words alone cannot describe, but I'll try. It was the beginning of 1989, and I had just turned fourteen.

The leaders of the home in Peru sent a group of us on a road trip to see other C.O.G homes in the area, where other second-generation teenagers lived. We traveled to the surrounding cities, towns, and countries. We were to be a beacon of light, an example of what teens in such a privileged home would be like. I was a miscreant, to say the least. My resentment was beginning to boil over. The more I woke up to my coming of age, the more I rebelled. The time bomb was ticking inside me.

One of the C.O.G homes we went to was in Chili. There was this gorgeous, young, second-generation teenage girl that I was very, very fond of. She lived in the home but had become friendly with a boy in the surrounding community. This boy's family owned a restaurant that would frequently give food to the home—we lived off the kindnesses of other people because of our mission and ministry in the world. The boy was not part of the organization. He was an outsider. It became obvious, to me anyway, that they were in love. The young girl eventually confided in me that she wanted the young boy. She thought that maybe her parents wanted her to convert him and bring him into the organization, so that they could be together. She seemed so scared and tired.

When the mission was over, I was sent back to the main teen home in Peru. I wrote letters to the young girl in Chili, as we were allowed to do. I encouraged her to not hide from her feelings. If she wanted to leave, then she should go be with him, instead of converting him to our organization. I was very passionate in my letters. I told her that things were not what they seemed. I just wanted her to feel that if she needed to, she could escape. She could be free with the boy she loved. Later, I would discover my letters to her were being intercepted.

Soon, my letters weren't all about her love story. Looking back, I was writing to myself, releasing my inner need to escape. (I never found out what happened to her or her first love.)

When I returned from Chili, there was a local construction worker who had been hired for property maintenance. We began to flirt. My desire for him grew intensely. This is when my need for approval from other men, women, girls, or boys—so I could love myself and find my true identity—had really kicked in.

He was an outsider. I wanted out. He was Peruvian, he was older. *This man had to know more than I did about the big world out there. He could show me....*

I would watch him, so devoted to his daily duties. His mind always seemed focused on the task at hand. He was sturdy like a rock. He could come to our quasi paradise, and then go home. He was a ghost. He was free. He was the exact opposite of me. He could see the world that we created and then walk away without anyone forbidding it.

He didn't have our indoctrination. He was a mystical creature in my world of concrete absolutes. He symbolized the outside world. There was no logic or reason behind that theory. There was only my subconscious pulling on me like gravity to earth, telling me I was destined to be free, like him. I longed for it every waking hour.

He wasn't even my type; I was more into girls. He was too old. But, he symbolized freedom. I thought about the young second-generation girl that I had encouraged to leave just a couple months prior. This Peruvian construction worker was my ticket out. I obsessed and fixated. I wore as few clothes as possible to try and seduce him. I just wanted him to fall in love with me. I wanted him to take me to a place far, far away.

One afternoon, the leaders of the organization called me into a private meeting. That's when the letters I wrote were brought up. Tears rolled down my cheeks. I felt immense betrayal. This was a meeting of exposure. They were exposing me for my rebellion, for the deeds I had been committing against them. They challenged me and said the young Peruvian construction worker had told them that he felt uncomfortable about "this young girl mesmerizing him." He indicated that he had a wife and children. He didn't know what to do about me; he felt awkward about the whole situation. The leaders asked me if I was trying to *flirty fish* him into the organization using my sexuality.

Another Mo Letter was entitled "Flirty Fishing." Christ's disciples were fishers of men (fishermen who would leave their boats to fish for other disciples). We, too, were to leave the safety of the C.O.G. and "fish" people out from the real world with the intent to convert them. The idea of flirtation was simple. Since sex was part of original innocence, being flirtatious with the outside world was a unique skill. Luring other people into our organization using sexual tactics was encouraged.

I'd been indoctrinated from the beginning, but, with the onset of puberty, I was starting to read between the lines. I began to become more self-aware. Certain triggers, like being told what to do, were causing impulsive reactions, even though I was not entirely aware of why. My personal feelings and my heart's desires were surfacing, too, even though I'd been trained not to have any. My innate value system, I was fast discovering, did not align with my surroundings. Every day I grew closer to adulthood, the walls of the C.O.G. moved ever close, suffocating me and becoming increasingly transparent. My extreme fear of getting pregnant and of never being able to freely connect with the world outside the organization became all consuming. Since I had traveled all my young life, I knew there was more out there. I had seen it, lived parallel to it. I had felt its sun warm my hair when I was small, when I longed for that dolly in the store window. I'd sang on its sidewalks, begging for money. I knew the noises of the real world; traffic and music and laughter. I'd felt its rain on my face and tasted it on my tongue. To the real world, I was just a visitor, a vacationer, a voyeur; yet, I knew it enough to yearn for it. At fourteen years old, between my memories, my surging personal beliefs, and this Peruvian construction worker, I was right there again—so close to the real world. My nose was pressed up against the glass partition separating it from me. But I had absolutely no power to reach out, to reach through the glass, to take my fist and smash it, to touch that world. I couldn't even go out and explore without supervision. Even when we did leave the compound in groups, it was always for their purpose, never for exploration or self-gratification.

In the C.O.G., we were perceived as simple tools to accomplish a mission. If that meant we had to use our bodies to seduce other outsiders to see our way of truth, then so be it. I was almost a woman now by their standards. So, what would stop my family from using me to fulfill the same mission and purpose? Who could help? There was no one.

I could not confess to flirty fishing, as I was not trying to lure the construction worker into the cult, but willing him to take me away from it…. Of course, I couldn't say that. I mostly just sat there mute, except for the sobbing. I was desperate. Freaked out. Scared as hell.

Later that day, after being confronted about the construction worker and my letters, I sat in one of the leader's bedrooms, sobbing. I could barely contain myself. I believe I had my first nervous breakdown that day. I remember it vividly. It was the day I realized I was not okay anymore. I was embarrassed for sending letters of betrayal to another girl, encouraging her to leave. On top of that, they took my obsession and twisted it, encouraging me to use my body to coerce that man to leave his wife and children, to join the organization and to cleave to me as a partner. (At least that was my fourteen-year-old perception.) What had I been doing with him? What was I thinking? In my soul I knew it was wrong, but I had no one to talk to, nowhere to turn. I was so lost.

I'd managed, between sobs, to tell the leader that I wanted to go home, back to Brazil. What that meant to me, I had no idea. The concept of a home was so foreign. Home was always a place of perpetual wandering. We seemed to always be fleeing from something: from persecution, or some other horror that the real world might do to us.

My father and brother came to mind. I wanted to get to them as fast as possible. If nothing else, I wanted to be as far away from the embarrassment of what was happening with the construction worker. And, I wanted to forget about my communication with the girl in Chili, too. These incidents were so big in my teenage brain. It felt as if I wouldn't be able to recover from them.

As soon as I told the leaders in Peru that I wanted to go home, they realized I wasn't trying to convert the construction worker. This, coupled with my letters, earned me a flight back to my father in Brazil as fast as they could dial the digits and book the ticket. They wanted me out of there. I was toxic—a backslider. I was a lost cause, unable to see the purpose and mission of their truth. Even worse, I'd encouraged that young girl to escape.

I had just seen one of our main leaders make out with numerous teens. I'd danced half naked with the other girls in the name of the sexual revolution in front of everyone. On one occasion, the leaders of the organization filmed all of us teenage girls dancing. We were draped in sheer scarves with no clothes underneath. This film footage was to be sent to Mo, our leader: "Grandpa" as was his latest moniker with third-generation babies being born of my peers. This was to be the proof that we embraced the sexual revolution; it was alive and thriving in the organization. *So what if we were children?* God had dictated that we were mature enough for exploitation. After all, if sex was not a sin, then what laws of the world could keep us from being free? This meant we could do anything to prove we were part of the sexual revolution....

Us girls, we just wanted to be accepted. We would do anything to prove our loyalty. To please the leaders, to prove our dedication to their mission and purpose; this is what we lived for. If they believed in us, we felt connected to God. To deny ourselves, our own rights and our wills at the expense of everything, also meant we were connected to God.

All my waking hours, it felt as if my heart, soul, and defense mechanisms were about to collapse. I could feel that ticking time bomb. I was at my wits end. And then I had the breakdown. My soul decided it no longer belonged to the organization. My soul was exercising free will for the first time ever.

A leader walked me to the airport. He told me he was placing a bet that in six months I'd be pregnant. Those were the last words I remember from my life in the Children of God cult. In that moment, a hatred I had never possessed before crept into my bones. That's when I met my shadow-self: the part that's capable of hatred, spite, and conscious anger. I wanted to slap his ill-gotten face and spit at his idealizations. All I could do was keep my head down and walk, staring at the ground.

That comment gave me all the fuel I needed to keep moving forward in those first weeks—to somehow find a life beyond the only reality I had ever known. In that regard, my shadow-self became my best friend. It wanted out of the organization more than anything. I wanted to prove that leader wrong. I wanted to prove him forever wrong. He would not control me. His prediction could not, would not, be my destiny.

I got on the plane and left the person I had been all my life with him. I was breaking out of my rusty cage. There was no concrete plan. I had no idea as to how I would find my freedom. All I knew was that my life could no longer exist in this dysfunctional state, in this sex-crazed, sadistic chaos.

I would soon discover that I hadn't magically entered the real world upon leaving this commune. I had punched my way through the glass wall. It was a start. But this new hatred that had seeped into my conscious like venom, like heroin, was tagging along. It would prove to be near-fatal as my teens years trudged on.

When I got back to my father, the first thing I asked was, "Where is my brother?" Dad said he'd gone back to America to be with our mother. I told him I wanted to go back to America, too. I hoped and prayed that he'd agree. After all, if he had let my brother go, then maybe he would let me go, too. I didn't want to explain anything. I didn't want to talk about anything. I figured he might have already known about what was happening and just didn't care. Whether that was true, I didn't have the strength to care. I just wanted to get the hell out of there as fast as my broken soul and crippled wings could take me. Would he let me go? Could I be so lucky?

My dad didn't have an emotional reaction regarding my brother's departure. And he never asked me why I wanted to leave, or what had caused me to shut down. Even though deep down I could tell he was sad about my brother and disturbed by my wishes, he was aloof, which seemed normal. I never remembered him truly caring about what we were feeling. Everything was secondary to the mission and purpose of the C.O.G. Many years later, I learned from a therapist about emotional incest: when a parent confides in their child as they would another adult, conveying their problems, or emotional needs as if their child can understand and help them through it. My father had done this his whole life, without ever wondering or inquiring about our emotional needs, our wellbeing.

Understanding this truth reinforced that my brother and I were tools, nothing more, nothing less. We were objects created to fulfill a purpose. There was no time for individuality or divergent thinking. There was no time to wonder about who we were as unique creations of the Divine. There was only us following the leader—the leader our dad loved and reverenced.

My brother's absence helped me to understand why I'd been chosen to go to the teen camp. I was a good girl. I would not cause any trouble. I was quiet. I was obedient. I would do whatever I was told. I had been conditioned well.

I thought about my brother and why he was left behind. I knew he'd always been a rebel. He would not pretend to be part of something he so disdained. He would wear his colors of red rebellion along with the scowl on his face. They hadn't broken him yet. I remember hoping they never would.

Maybe it was easier to grant him that wish with me gone. Maybe the leaders were concerned he'd poison me and, I, too, would create "problems." Maybe other kids would catch on. Maybe they feared a teenage revolution. I'll never really know.

As far as I knew, Dad wasn't informed of the letters I'd sent to the girl. He didn't know about the construction worker, either. But, since so many of us children were growing into young teenagers, there was this sense of urgency to ensure that dissenters, or rebels like my brother and me, were not allowed to poison the rest of the group. We were told that all it takes is "one rotten apple to spoil the whole barrel full" (Isaiah 65:8). So, if we were to choose another path, or speak out, or ask questions, we were deemed toxic to the group.

• • •

When it became clear that I wanted to leave, I was considered a shame to the organization. I was kept in a room away from the other members, so as not to intoxicate them with my lies, deceit, and backsliding. But, by that time, it was too late; I was very, very promiscuous. I hit on all the adult men that came to bring me my daily food. I took showers out in the open area to tantalize them, hoping they would see me.

I was determined to shame them the same way they were shaming   me. I would use their own ideology against them. They said that sex was not a sin. I was determined to prove it. I would give myself to anyone that I chose, even in my rebellion. What would they do to me? What could they do to me that they hadn't already done? What could they take away from me? I would give my body away relentlessly. After all, wasn't this what they taught me? Wasn't this the education that was crucial to my development as a disciple?

It was a taste of their own medicine. Toxic. Just as they said I would be. In my own demise, they would see their reflection and weep. I looked at myself as if I were an illusion. I no longer felt real.

It all happened so organically. The natural planes of my consciousness were enraptured in all this cyclical madness. I had come full circle, facing off with my inner demons. I was my own demise. I was their worst nightmare. I was what they had created. I was what they refused to see. I was the forbidden fruit that would not so easily rot. I was a fighter, but not the kind they wanted.

None of the men that came with things like food, clothing, and bedding did anything sexual with me. One of the guys took some pictures, but he never touched me. They were afraid. I was too divergent. They feared I'd say something or do something that might cause others to think about leaving. Maybe they feared whatever had erupted inside me—thought it a contagion. They were terrified of me, of my power, of their creation. I was an animal, albeit a caged one. I imagine some of them viewed me a display—a wonder to see, but don't get too close to the tiger for it could pounce. It will pounce. And they were terrified I might engage them in dialogue. This lasted for a week, maybe two. It was during these days that my true innocence died: I became numb. I detached myself from my past and my existence. I no longer perceived myself as a young girl. I had become nothing. I was no one.

I remember, the evening after my return, looking out the window and seeing my dad with his shirt off, doing some yardwork like nothing had happened. I'm sure he was wrestling with his inner demons. After all, my brother and I were both dissenters, which reflected poorly on him. I imagine he just wanted to remain in the organization's good graces, so he had to follow suit, to prove his loyalty. To remind them that he was still going to follow God and our leader no matter what he lost in the process—no matter what he had to forsake.

When I asked to leave, my father must have worked something out with the organization like he had done for my brother. I'm not sure how he figured out my mother's telephone number, but I think he got it from his mother, our grandmother. He allowed me to leave the grounds with him, to call my mother.

I kept trying to imagine what home meant. I had no memories from which to draw, but since my brother was already there, I couldn't imagine her telling me no. Our father told me that she had remarried a lawyer. That was all I knew.

All I remember saying on the phone was, "Hi, Mom, it's me, your daughter. I want to come home." Later, my mother told me she was terrified that I was pregnant. Regardless, she paid for the ticket to America, just as she had done for my brother.

That was in 1989, right at the tail end of summer, right before the new school year started.

Chapter

7

WHEN I LANDED IN CALIFORNIA, I got off the plane and took the escalator to baggage claim along with the rest of the passengers. There were many people waiting below, but one woman caught my attention. Somehow, I knew she was my mother, even though I hadn't seen her since I was three. When our eyes met, she knew who I was, too. The closer I got, the colder and more distant the space between us became. This was my first memory in my new world, my first jolt of freedom. It felt intensely cold.

In retrospect, I can understand it. I was experiencing her pain. I was an illusion to her, just as she was to me. Here I was—her daughter. But I was not her daughter. She didn't know me. She only saw me through the vacant lens of what she remembered the organization to be. I was their fruit. I was the product of something she had created a long time ago, something she had tried to forget.

She had been separated from my brother and me, had escaped from the organization and, by default, from us. And here I was. It appeared, even in those first moments, that my existence was too much for her to bear.

Many years before I arrived in California, she had tried to find my brother and me in South America. She had searched desperately with no success. Maybe she gave up the search after that, just to maintain her sanity and peace of mind.

We walked to her car. On the way to my new home, she outlined the ground rules. At that point, I was no longer what I would describe as a true human being. I was lost, clouded in my reason and judgment. I had no soul that I could feel. I had no clarity of mind. I just wanted to see my brother and be left alone to let the anger roll inside me like a thunderstorm. I wanted to believe there was some kind of divergent freedom out there somewhere with my biological mother; yet, deep down, I knew that was a pipe dream. I imagine my brother felt the same way. We were not self-aware. We had no one to talk to about this; no one to comfort us. And, to make matters stranger, with all the sexual encounters I had experienced, the day I was sent to my freedom in the real world was the day I started my menstrual cycle. I had no one to talk to about that, either. I was dirty and broken. My mind was crazed and blurry. My reality was clouded with ambiguity and the unknown.

My brother had been there for several months. It was like hitting puberty had pushed us both over the edge. I believe that's why we both ran screaming before something really terrifying happened.

My brother had already begun to wreak havoc in Northern California. He was a teenage boy. Utterly disturbed. He was running himself wild; he was scared and scarred beyond belief. He didn't care about consequences. He took his freedom by the horns and rode it recklessly. I stood by watching, wondering, and occasionally cheering him on in those first few weeks home.

I was put into public school days after my arrival. I sat for my freshman yearbook picture like any other normal student and managed to smile just enough to hide my soullessness with a bit of hope, or so I prayed. I look at that picture of myself now; it's hanging on my wall. I look at that shallow smile. Her skin was beautiful. She was perfect, physically. The girl in the picture was youthful. I look deeper into her eyes somedays, and see that she was still hopeful that an opportunity existed for her to be different by becoming the same as everyone else, by becoming normal, by blending in. All she wanted was to see life through different lenses like the other kids, exchange her Children of God reality for the new one before her. But it was too late.

I was not youthful. I was damaged. I was broken. I was tired. I was scared. I, too, was scarred. And the worst thing about it was that I wasn't self-aware enough to process those feelings. I didn't know how to adjust. How to behave. I was simply reactive.

I think about how I was conditioned and taught to relate to myself, to God, and to the world around me. My animal-self was disconnected. I was going from a world of seclusion to a world of non-seclusion with newfound freedom. I had no idea what to do with that freedom. The adjustment period was arduous. Every waking moment felt like a lie. I was a lie. I worked to hide my true self, even though I didn't know what that was, or where it was. So, what was I hiding? I knew not my true self, other than the girl that was raised in a sex cult. That wasn't my choice, that wasn't me. I was raised to believe there was no me. And, then, like blinking, I was in a world where people had individual identities that mattered to them. That meant something. Identities they protected and cultivated.

I was the result of intense brainwashing. I was an animal by nature, but I was still a being of consciousness—the similitude of a human in the beginnings of discovering awareness, which wouldn't happen until much, much later. Many religious textbooks and other spiritual books tell us that we need to suppress our animal self. Like the ego, we need to control it. Put it under subjection. That had already been my entire existence to date. I needed to discover my inner animal and then learn how to manage it.

Some might argue that my animal-self, along with nature/nurture, was responsible for the promiscuity—and hitting puberty was a part of that. But, it wasn't the nudity or the sex in general that I had been exposed to that had triggered my mental breakdown. It was the master manipulation of my life, personal identity, and will. And my early sexual experiences blurred the lines between what it meant to be a child versus an adult. This made it that much worse. Acclimating to being a kid in this new world was impossible. I had been encouraged to have no will of my own up to that point, I was left wide open: easy prey. And because of it, I was never a kid.

My animal instinct to survive is what had set me free. But, because my brain was not fully developed, I was not aware that my end goal was to thrive. At the age of fourteen, I only knew to survive—at the least by not getting pregnant. That was my singular goal, with no other goals in the queue.

I had been driven by my fear of giving birth. My body was still so small and not completely grown yet. It makes perfect sense to me now. Looking back, I ran fast and furious from my greatest fear. Ironically, I ended up running right into a new set of dangers, which I was unprepared to face.

I can be objective now that my sexual experiences with the young girls no longer bothers me. They were a natural part of my adolescence. But back then I wasn't kind to myself. I was burdened by these horrible secrets. Everyone was perfect, except me. I was the young girl who'd never had the opportunity to think for herself or play and laugh like normal girls. With so many normal kids around me, with so many people to hide from in the new world, it was too overwhelming.

I had no identity, no "real" past from which to draw to carry me through adolescence and into adulthood. It was tearing my soul apart. I was hiding all these things that had happened to me. I buried them like a pet in the backyard, but without a ceremony or any loving words. But without these things that had happened to me, I was no one.

I was nothing.

There are times I can still feel the energy of my teenage self. I can feel the passion, the lust, the fever of confusion, the longing for clarity. The difference now is I understand it.

Chapter

8

MOSES DAVID WAS A MAN who took many lovers on his road to revolution. His original wife was not subservient enough to his mission and purpose, so they separated. I was not privy to the details, but, she, and at least one of his other daughters, left him when he founded the organization. David Brant Berg, "Moses David" to the cult, found a more malleable bride.

In order to paint this next picture clearly, it's important to remember the era I was born into was one of revolution. The Beatles were singing of such ideologies. The Vietnam War triggered a separation of people who wanted to rebel—against war, against the status quo, against anything else that was a part of the "establishment."

The Children of God organization was birthed in the early 1970s as a result of the wave of people, especially youth, that were disillusioned with the types of conformity that would create war vs. peace.

Moses David capitalized on those people.

Maybe it started as a sincere desire to help the lost hippie generation. Maybe it was his obsession with the Bible and his Evangelical background that gave him a platform from which to easily build upon. Maybe it was timing.

He believed he could create a new type of hippie culture that still held itself true to the ideals of freedom and free love, but in the context of following a representation of Jesus and the Bible. He wanted the security of knowing his ideas were based on something real and true. Free love for the sake of free love was fun but flighty. Free love in the name of Jesus Christ—there was everlasting power in that.

He could use the Bible as his alibi and Jesus as his own personal witness of truth. Still, to this day, I try to believe that his heart was pure and his desires sincere; that he wanted to help a lost and lonely generation find peace amidst the chaos of war; that he was trying to usher in a new era, one of love.

But, Moses David had a fascination with leaders like Castro, the dictator of Cuba. He, himself, became a dictator. One who believed that God, through Jesus Christ, was guiding him. Who can argue when someone claims to have a direct connection to the Almighty? Where is the place where human error is recognized? When you have so much power that you tailor-made a subservient flock, who among them could be brave enough to question anything?

I can see how that era created opportunity for its youth to find peace and solace in the form of spirituality. I can see how being considered an outcast could be enticing, especially one that had purpose, was following the Creator. They could be "dropouts," and still feel a sense of comradery, family, have a place to call home. Mo provided a way for these lonely youth to be crazy, wild, and revolutionary; to burn their old ideas along with their bras; to be free from drugs and street life but hold true to their inner rebel against what they called "The System." And he created this utopia in the name of Jesus.

The "Church System" was something they all rebelled against. In that rebellion, out of the "mouth of God" via Mo, a liberal faith that was nonconforming and purely derivative was birthed.

To elucidate the degree of nonconformity and rebellion, the direct line of cause and effect must be drawn.

There was a time when the revolution began that women were used as tools to get men to give them donations, such as money or other things. There was a Mo Letter called "Whores for Jesus." There was another one I mentioned earlier called "Flirty Fishing." On the cover of this letter was a picture of a very sexy woman sitting on a fisherman's hook because women were bait. We were to use our sexuality and provocative nature to catch men. The Bible says that we should be fishers of men because many of Christ's disciples were fishermen. So, this interpretation was that women or men could be used to fish other people into the Kingdom of God using their sexual prowess. Remember, sex was not considered to be a sin in this group. Sex was part of original innocence; therefore, it was easy to propose use of our sexuality to provoke others to follow our mission and purpose. Being a "whore" in the name of Jesus was encouraged. That was literally their terminology.

The new bride that Mo took was instructed to go out into the world to capture such a fish. She did so, successfully becoming pregnant with what the leaders referred to as a "Jesus baby" because he was the product of her "winning over" a man to Jesus Christ. This man was of Latin origin, and so she named her son, Davidito. It meant "little David" in Spanish. He was to be thought of as a successor to Moses David's throne—a young prophet of the End Times.

It was a foolproof plan, one that surely couldn't fail as the plan that my father had for my brother and me did. Moses David was much stronger than my father, who was just a number, really, one of thousands in his flock.

Davidito was going to be groomed to reign.

Chapter

9

DAVIDITO WAS A FEW YEARS younger than me. It's likely he had not yet hit puberty when I first began to recognize and understand who he was, which was some kind of Children of God demi-god, or a prince to Mo's self-ordained kingship.

As this young boy grew up with this leader and his wife, he was an experiment of a certain kind. His nannies had been encouraging Davidito to explore his sexuality. The leaders wanted to know what would happen if a child were conditioned without shame to explore their sexual nature from a young age. There were articles written about it. Not everyone was able to access those documents. I happened to stumble upon one of them at the teen home one day. It was a "black book" that had been left out accidentally. Many of the words had been blacked out, but from what I could read and understand, Davidito was playing sexually with at least one of his nannies or another female in their home. As I read the entries, I was not surprised at all. I knew it was true.

This young boy was prophesied to be a great leader in the End Times. It was predicted he would have massive powers that would come from God. He and another young woman would fight the Antichrist and lead us to victory when the Devil took over humanity in an effort to destroy the world.

Davidito never had a life of his own. He was taught, just like my brother and me, to be yielding. We were to sign a blank sheet of paper and do whatever God, through these leaders, told us to do. Everything was arranged.

I never got to meet Davidito, but he was popular among us teenagers. He was seen as a role model. He was practically royalty. He would be the one to inherit the mantel of success after Mo and his bride passed on.

To my knowledge, none of the other second-generation teenagers were allowed to meet him until well after puberty (but I don't know this for absolute fact). Davidito, to our knowledge, lived in hiding with Berg, his bride, and two other children. He wasn't allowed any other friends. He wasn't allowed to experience even the small and limiting freedoms the rest of us did. I always wondered why Mo and his bride were always hiding. I wondered why Davidito couldn't come out and get to know the other second-generation children and adults. I assumed he was too important—too holy for us to see or communicate with. He was that godlike or so we were told, and God could not be seen by the naked eye.

The extent of these prophecies grew when the organization came out with a comic book called *Heaven's Girl*. We were introduced to it around 1986. "Heaven's Girl" was a sexy, young, scantily clad girl with a black braid. She held a staff in her hands that carried magical powers. She was illustrated many times with a young boy alongside her that looked like a teenage Davidito. He was portrayed as her sidekick. He was written as one of the End-time prophets in the series. He would speak God's word into the sky and Antichrist planes would be shot down in droves with lightning and fire from the heavens. They would hide Christians and save them from certain death.

It was the closest thing to magic we'd ever been exposed to. There was so much that made us feel powerful and closer to God, but this comic book was the pinnacle of effective propaganda. It was my favorite. It made the young teenager in me feel empowered, like I could do anything, just like this girl with the powers. But, there was always a darker side to things, which involved mind control and sex.

One of the comic books that came out described a story wherein Heaven's Girl was caught by a group of Antichrist soldiers. In the Bible, there is a story about a man named Daniel. In the story, he resisted his king and was thrown into a lion's den to be eaten alive. In this comic book, Heaven's Girl was thrown into a tomb. There were lions everywhere. She knelt down and prayed. The lions did not eat her alive. They did not leave her carcass there to rot, like all of the other men and women who had been cast into this dungeon. This was apparent—that dozens of people had been eaten—by the piles of leftover bones in the illustrations. When she was finally released from the lion's den unscathed but with a dress that was thin, shredded, and transparent, soldiers began to gang rape her. Her outfit was a magnet for rape. But, in this gang rape illustration, she was praying for the souls of her rapists to be saved—even as she was being raped.

As I had mentioned, my hormones were off the charts. I was without any sexual boundaries. But seeing this frightening scene confused me sexually and petrified me to death. To imagine that such a violation of my body could actually happen was inconceivable. But that was the message.

I remember enjoying my sexual freedom, while simultaneously being terrified of the consequences of being so open to sex, especially at a pre-pubescent age. In reading all the letters and the comics, I thought my destiny must be to breed, bring life into a world I didn't belong to. It made no sense.

Davidito was perceived like Heaven's Girl. He was an End-time warrior. We were all in awe. We wanted that opportunity. To be that important to the mission. To be seen as something more than a disciple. We were nothing and he was something. We all wanted to be like Davidito. Like Heaven's Girl. They were mighty and strong. Heaven's Girl wasn't real, but she was powerful in all the ways we desired and strove to be. She and Davidito were two "tactics" they used to make us want to stay in the organization. Using kids to brainwash other kids is a very effective tool.

Even though the idea of the end of the world was scary, if we got to be on the side of God and have magical powers to destroy our enemies, well, that was a pretty good deal. Striving to be godlike, to be like Davidito our warrior child and like Heaven's Girl from the comic book, kept many of our minds focused for some time.

I spoke about self-will and how our identities were never a topic of focus. We were merely tools on a mission to fulfill our purpose. There was an enormous amount of pressure on Davidito to fulfill the prophecy, to fulfill this role he would play in the foretold events—to be the prophet of all mankind, a savior at the end of the world. Can you imagine the pressure? Plus, his isolation? Plus, being taught (trained) to explore his sexuality from a very young age?

Around the year 2000, roughly eighteen years after I left the organization, I was watching the news one day. This was after I'd moved to Oregon from California by Divine providence. A picture of Davidito appeared in one of the news stories. I would've recognized him anywhere. He looked exactly the same as he had in all the photos we had studied and worshiped over the years. He was that same boy in this photo on the news, just an older version. However, Davidito was no prophet as it turned out. He was on the news because he'd had a liaison with one of his nannies (or another elder female) out in the real world. During that encounter, he murdered her.

I got on YouTube and watched the video of his last minutes on earth. He had videotaped himself for an hour before committing these crimes, exposing the terrifying abuses he had suffered at the hands of the Children of God cult. Not only was he abused, but he had been witness to one of the young girls taken repeatedly to Berg's bed in the middle of the night. He witnessed the leaders "beating the Devil" out of other teens in his home. He talked about the bruises another young girl had from these violent episodes with the leaders of the organization. He had also been to a teen camp, like I had. He talked about his inner rage. He had a gun in his hand and was filling it with bullets. He had military knives. He said he wouldn't get his mother or her leader lover, but he would get "one of them"—someone who had wronged him—and justice would be served. He looked like an assassin. After shooting that YouTube video, he went and killed one of the elder females. He found justice the only way he knew how. He stabbed her to death in bloody revenge, and then he shot himself in the head.

Later, I found an online interview with a news broadcaster and one of the members of the organization. This member was saying that all of the things people had heard about the C.O.G. were lies. Lies told by their enemies. I knew then, for certain, that they were the liars. I knew it was all true. Davidito had been abused. I remembered the past more clearly in that instance than I ever had. It made my heart tremble with incredible fear all over again.

Davidito's survival instincts had taken over. He was confused. Angry. He had spent his entire life in captivity. Abuse and brainwashing were a way of life for him. I know his childhood was even worse than mine. I can't imagine. None of that makes it right. But the inner turmoil he must've felt, separating himself from the only thing he had ever known to face a world he had been told was pure evil—it must have been too much. He couldn't make it work. He couldn't make sense of it. He couldn't find himself on the outside. He couldn't find love. He had never had love, so how could he recognize it? He broke. They set out to destroy our souls and our individuality from the moment of our birth, and they succeeded in the case of Davidito. What else could he do? He sought revenge, he sought freedom. He got both.

Of course, the leaders would call him possessed, say that the Devil was trying to bring their organization down with more persecution. What were they to say to defend themselves?

What I saw was a young boy who'd been abused and exposed to adult experimentation. His life was sheltered. Everything he was allowed to see or experience was dictated by his adoptive father, our leader, and by his mother. He was only exposed to events or ideas that served them and their agenda. His life was predicted for him without any consent or will of his own.

I can't imagine that he was given any choices. They might've given him the illusion of free will, but always with the notion that he would choose what they wanted. I doubt they ever cared about what he wanted or who he was or what his talents were.

He sought revenge because everything, including his identity, had been lost in the groupthink and predestination of this organization. He took back his power through violence.

What did this act of revenge do to him? It killed him. He had nothing left to live for. He had no real power. His crime and subsequent suicide was a symbol of taking the power back. All he wanted was to find himself. All he wanted was to no longer be their slave—oftentimes, their sex slave.

Thinking about it now, my heart breaks for Davidito. He would have made a great marine or humanitarian soldier fighting against the evils of the world, protecting children. I know he had a kind spirit. You could see his spirit and feel his pain in his last moments on earth.

I know that kids experiment with their sexuality when they are young. Usually it's with kids their own age. There are no words to explain how confusing it is when you are a child that's expected to experiment sexually with adults. They are your role models. They have all the power—the power to shame you. To discipline you. To give you grace. To provide for you. To give you direction. Every child has the innate desire to please those who rule over them. Disappointing our parents and guardians is a hard thing to face. This makes children ideal victims for abusers.

I believe this is exactly what caused Davidito to snap. They got the answer to their Bible-driven, separatist, mind-controlling, sexual experiment—all of this, in the name of love. They'd created a murderer, a true lost soul, incapable of real love, unable to forgive, unequipped to live in the "real" world.

When I see violent crimes take place at the hands of teens like the Columbine shooters and so many others since, I can't help but wonder what abuse or neglect the perpetrators might've endured to cause that kind of outrage. Were they bullied? Were their parents neglectful and absent? Were they raped or molested? Were they physically, emotionally, or psychologically abused? Were they stuck in front of the TV, exposed to violence at an early age without an adult to help them navigate and process the reality and dangers of life as their cognitive brains developed? Were they witness to violence as the norm? I know there are a percentage of killers that have come from normal families and there is no excuse for them, but environmental abuse at a young age increases the likelihood of

violent behavior to manifest in adulthood by fifty percent (https://www.ncbi.nlm.nih.gov/pmc/articles/PMC539471/).

I'm afraid of, but also feel connected to, children that are so lost they resort to violence. What could provoke them to feel so much evil that their psychotic breaks could be so deadly? I'm lucky to have never experienced that kind of violent break. Later in life, during times of my greatest dysfunction, my rage was mainly directed inward. I did get into fights with my brother and girls at school, but I never killed anyone. I did try to kill myself once or twice or maybe three times....

Now, I feel lucky that the revenge I seek is not in the form of violence toward the guilty. My free will is not interested in perpetrating random acts of violence on innocent people, either. It's not in me to hurt others as I have been hurt. The innocent should never be punished, even at the hands of victims of violence of the like.

I've found power and revenge in forgiveness. It's hard, painful, and easier said than done at times. I still feel anger and rage when a memory surfaces. The sting of awareness can arise from an innocent, everyday occurrence, reminding me I'm different; I come from someplace else. But, every day I strive to achieve forgiveness toward those who've wronged my brother and me and other children like us, and every night I go to bed grateful.

As an educated, worldly woman, I recognize that my young mind had been manipulated by a psychic frenzy. And, although I rejected this conditioning and was able to escape, my subconscious remained captive. This created inner turmoil, discontent, and compulsive self-doubt, which turned into rage that I mainly unleashed upon myself.

In the writing of this book and the living of my life, I remember this scripture daily. "If your enemy is hungry, give him food to eat; And if he is thirsty, give him water to drink; For you will heap burning coals of fire on his head, and the Lord will reward you" (Proverbs 25:22).

Chapter

10

A FEW YEARS BACK, AFTER I obtained my license to teach K–12, I attended a training to teach youth in prison (ages twelve to twenty-five). Some of these kids had committed violent crimes, some of those crimes were sexual offenses, and some had been tried as adults. During that training, I learned about the amygdala, which is the lower part of the brain that governs emotion and impulse—primal instinct. Most young people operate under the guidance of this region. Contrarily, the frontal lobe—which doesn't fully develop until about age twenty-five—governs the concepts of logic, reason, and consequence.

Over 50 percent of youth in the prison system have been abused. Using a platform of prior conditioning that was hardwired into their brains, they operated on impulse and emotion, not understanding the consequences of their actions. Even when consequences were mapped out, they no longer had enough humanity left to care. Many operated without rationalizing their crime(s) before committing them. And, they were so used to suffering, to expect to suffer, they became numb to the pain of others, as well.

When abuse is severe and repetitive, the impulse to act out in ways that are destructive increases. Impulse vs. awareness. The victim becomes the victimizer when impulse wins.

I mentioned before that within days of arriving in California, I was put in a public school. Neither my brother nor I had any clue how to behave. Our lives had always been dictated for us. We had repressed so much pain for so long due to our conditioning, we didn't know how to manage it in the regular world. Our modes of coping were not healthy; we lashed out verbally and physically; we drank, smoked, experimented with drugs, and the list goes on. We acted like lions, in that we gave off alpha vibes. Even the look in our eyes appeared calm and steady like a lion's. Except, we didn't know how to live in our new jungle, which made us easy prey. We'd come off like the kind of kids you didn't want to fuck with, but then end up the victim by every new scenario's end.

In finding our freedom, we became perpetual victims, as we didn't understand how to exercise our free will appropriately or work through our pain.

Imagine a child walking down the sidewalk hand in hand with his mother. Now imagine he's got a head wound and it's bleeding. Now, imagine his mother is ignoring it, the child is ignoring it, everyone is. If you saw this for real on a city street, you'd pinch yourself, thinking you were dreaming. In real life, someone would ask if this child is okay. Another person might stop and yell at the mother for ignoring the wound. My brother and I bled from the head for years in the cult, as they held our hands and read us their stories. We were blinded by blood, choking on it, while everyone pretended everything was okay. This happened because we didn't matter. It was the movement that mattered, not the individual. We left the cult with these bloody head wounds. I didn't expect the real world to notice, as they weren't looking for it. But, surely, I thought my mother would have recognized that we were bleeding and needed comfort....

My brother and I each had separate, psychotic breaks early into our freedom. He became violent in school. He had no respect for other people's girlfriends, for one thing. He was a taker. He tried desperately to get his power back by coveting girls that appeared to be desirable by the most basic fact that they were taken. We had never experienced maternal affection of any kind. Maybe that's what he saw in a typical high school relationship. Teenagers have a lot of energy and sexual energy; it could have been as simple as that. He was around other hormonal teenagers all day and craved the kind of attention, affection, love he saw other boys his age receiving from their girlfriends. The fights never seemed to end. He was an attractive person and intriguing because he was different, "off." As you can imagine that only made things worse.

My psychotic break caused self-harm more than anything. I felt weak and powerless. I was naïve. I was care-less; I cared about nothing. I was apathetic. I was suicidal. I was promiscuous. I had little respect for other people's sexual boundaries, that included other girls' boyfriends. I had been brainwashed to believe I was nothing and that my body was for the taking. With the apathy came a sense that I might be evil. A toothache generally doesn't go away unless you go to the dentist and have it taken care of. That's what the evil inside me felt like. It was a dull ache that never fully subsided. I used to think that if I died it would go away. In death I will be free of the ache inside my heart and the rot inside my brain. It was a sick and pathetic thing, my existence back then as a fourteen-year-old girl.

Our destiny as dissenters had been foretold by Moses David. We would be like all the other backsliders. We would end up being destroyed by the world. Destroyed by the Devil's playground. My brother and I fell into self-fulfilling prophecies with no effort at all. We fell into the fires of hell of which we'd been warned.

During those first days with my mother, despite being confused, lost, and scared, I knew one thing: Despite feeling crippled and insecure compared to my peers, I didn't want to go back to the cult. However, the indoctrination, the brainwashing, it was following me like a shadow. All I wanted to do was escape it, but I didn't know how.

I see all of this so clearly now, but back then I only understood bits and pieces. Nothing was concrete. I existed in body, but I was nonexistent in awareness. I saw my own reflection, but my reflection was not me. My eyes that appeared strong and steady to others, my lion eyes, they were hollow to me and tired from life.

As soon as I managed to creep out of my shell long enough to make an acquaintance or two, I found drugs. Some kids were hanging out in a van that was parked outside school on the route home. They stopped me and said they wanted me to try something. They said, "Stick out your tongue." They placed what looked like a tiny piece of paper on it. They told me to hold it in my mouth but don't swallow.

The following morning, I was supposed to go on a trip with my Spanish class to Mexico. That night, I told my newly found friends that I needed to go home. The LSD didn't hit me until later. It was crazy; I had never felt so wonderful in my entire life. All I wanted to do was take off all my clothes and stand in front of my mirror and dance naked. I managed to get my stuff ready and pack for the trip somehow.

My stepdad gave me a ride to school at dawn. I sat in the car for what felt like hours, trying to keep myself composed while waiting for the bus to arrive. The trees danced in the wind. I thought they were talking to me. Or dancing for me. I don't know how I managed to not "break character" and bust out laughing. My survival instincts had kicked in. I imagined he would kill me if he found out. So, I played it cool.

When those strangers put that piece of paper on my tongue, I experienced an alternative reality that was so incredible, so mesmerizing, words still cannot explain it. Things went from drab and dreary to colorful and vibrant, like a rainbow. The sky no longer cried and bled for me. It danced. It sang. It embraced me. It called me into a world of wonder and magic so powerful that I never wanted to go home to the gray place I had known. What home could transcend this experience of freedom? I had only known pain. Now, I saw something brighter on the horizon: I was a part of the song and dance of life, as opposed to existing parallel to it. And the trees, they were dancing for me.

But, on the road to Mexico the waves of color faded. The rainbow died, and there I was again, existing alone.

From that day onward, I looked for drugs every waking moment. I hated reality. It was cold, cruel, and confusing. Oddly, life made more sense when I was disconnected from it.

From what was I trying to escape? Because of my choice to leave and rebel, I was doomed to fail miserably in life, to end up lost or dead...as was predicted.

I just wanted to be liberated from the belief that I was evil, and drugs seemed like the only way.

Chapter

11

MY MOTHER TRIED TO EMBRACE my brother and me. She wanted to give us everything. She gave us all the material things we'd never had and tried to include us in family events. My father had taken us away from her. This was her chance to make up for that, a chance to release her guilt and pain. She provided the illusion of a sanctuary and we were grateful, but we didn't know how to show it. Looking back, I see one basic truth: she was no more emotionally available for this adventure than we were. Helping us heal meant reopening wounds and rendering herself vulnerable to memories of her cult days.

Even though she no longer believed in the choice she'd made to join the C.O.G., she was an adult at the time of joining. No one had forced her; it didn't go against her will. She and my father thought they'd found nirvana. Their intentions were pure. They wanted to see the world through different eyes because conformity was failing them, and they'd lost all sense of peace.

I imagine she felt enormous guilt over joining the cult, agreeing to have children within their walls, and then abandoning them upon the request of my father.

She had tried to track us down in Brazil at various times in the early 1980s. I vaguely remember our father telling us something about someone coming after us. *The law, maybe?* I didn't know for sure because it felt like we were always running. And I remember seeing newspaper articles. And then her quest ended. She gave up, believing she would never find us.

She told me she had hoped we would come to her—that being with her was a dream come true, was her prayers being answered. Except her beautiful eyes showed no emotion and were absent of tears of joy or any other kind whenever we'd try and talk about this. To manage the pain of losing us for ten years, she'd shut off her feelings—at least enough to survive. She, too, wanted so desperately to thrive. She had rebuilt everything. She wanted to provide a good life for the baby she'd escaped with, our little sister. She had remarried a man who was nothing like our father. He was a lawyer— honest and true. He came from a good family, a military family. He was strict, but also kind. He was secure, stable, handsome. He was benevolent. He had compassion for our mother and her past. He loved her despite the baggage. He conformed but in the most productive and genuine way. He had no idea what we would bring to their doorstep.

Thinking about this transition in our lives makes my heart hurt. My mother had been resilient. She'd created paradise anew. She can't have known her two oldest children would be the deadly storm that would annihilate it all.

We were strangers.

Right after we arrived, our stepdad lost his job working as a partner at a bank. Now, he had two more children than he'd planned, and he had to rebuild his career as a lawyer. Meanwhile, our mom tried to heal us, but her guilt and shame prevented her from seeking outside assistance, from talking about the unthinkable truths from her past in order to break beyond them...to save us. And so, we all perished in the aftermath.

Chapter

12

THE PSYCHOLOGICAL, EMOTIONAL, AND SEXUAL abuse came from our environment, but the physical abuse was at the hands of our father. I believe my father didn't know any better; he was just doing what had been done to him.

One time we were on a road trip. It had to be around 1980. I was probably six, my brother five. We were traveling like gypsies, preaching the gospel in Brazil. As I mentioned before, my father had no income, so he relied on his faith and on the graces of other people to support us with donations on our journey.

We had stopped at a restaurant due to car trouble. There was smoke pouring out of the hood. My father's wife (not by legal marriage, but by mutual union) was sitting quietly, as she always did, in the front seat.

My father had a screwdriver and was feverishly attempting to fix the car. He had neither the money nor the resources to take it to a mechanic. I imagine we were not close to one, either, or he might've provisioned repairs. (That's what getting donated resources was called.)

My brother and I were fighting in the back seat. We had been traveling for days or maybe even months with barely, if any, toys, books, or playtime. We were mandated to silence during trips. "Enjoy the ride" is what he'd say. But we couldn't sit still. We were stir-crazy.

My father was angry at the stupid car for not working. Our arguing only made it worse. He came to the back window and asked us if we wanted a knuckle sandwich. My brother was closest to him so he received the blow. My father still had the screwdriver in his hand. When he gave my brother a knuckle sandwich, the screwdriver hit his head. It began to bleed—heavily. I was so scared.

Our father was horrified and remorseful. He stopped the bleeding, found a bandage, and put it on the wound that had soiled my brother's beautiful, blond hair.

Going forward, there were spankings. They fell mostly on my brother. My father's spankings were strategic. He had mastered the art of the spanking. He used belts, hangers, wooden paddles, or whatever branches we'd find in the back yard or woods. We did a lot of camping, so the forest never failed to produce the right stick. It was the only way my father knew how to regain control and provoke the behaviors he desired. It drove knives into my brother's soul. And then it made him stronger than hell. It was not healthy for my father, either. Sometimes, he would cry afterwards and try to rationalize his behavior. He would plead with us to behave so he didn't have to be violent again. After getting spanked, despite his sore ass, my brother would clench his fists and scowl, like he was burning with determination to fight and resist all punishment—to survive the trauma of it all.

When he became a teen that resistance continued. This was long before we left the organization and our father. My brother started rejecting all authority and always wound up in deep trouble because of it. He became hard, cold, and jaded. Yet, he gleamed of such an angelic essence that even when he would hide his smile, he still glowed. I swear he had an "It" factor just like a movie star. Who knew what was on his mind? Who knew what was going on in his soul?

Predictably, those behavioral issues carried over when we moved in with our mother. We were a couple of ticking time bombs. Nobody knew how to detonate us. Nobody even tried.

When we settled in, our worlds revolved around school, making new friends, finding boyfriends, girlfriends, and discovering drugs. Now that I understand what statutory rape is, I could accuse many boys of this crime. I was always attracted to older boys and few cared about my age. It was the reverse, really; it turned them on. I don't know why I did it. Maybe I thought they had the answers I was looking for. Maybe I thought they could give me something I craved.

I never thought of myself as being a pretty girl, but it was obvious that both boys and girls were attracted to me—like bees to honey. I came from a sexually promiscuous organization. I didn't have boundaries. I didn't have pretenses. I didn't even understand what a "reputation" was, not that it would've mattered, but I certainly wasn't trying to be known as a good girl or a bad girl. I was just a kid that wanted a normal life, normal parents; I wanted to be happy and experience love.

My whole life had been built on "if they want it, give it to them." Now that I was free, I wanted to take everything in this new world. I wanted all the attention. I wanted all the escape. I wanted to feed my hunger and obsessions. I wanted to find myself in the illusion of pleasure as long as it helped me forget everything I was, everything I'd become.

I know sexuality is a part of who we are. After all, we learn more about ourselves through our shared experiences with others. Adults who are in tune with who they are can experience intimacy in a way that's healthy.

My point is that I was still a child. My brain was not fully developed. I had no self-identity. I had been taken advantage of by so many adults in the cult. I was fighting for my self-esteem. My will. My true self. I was looking for my wings. Where were they? If I had any recognition of who I really was, I would've loved myself enough to choose boys or girls that would've loved me in return, or, at the very least, ones who would have understood and cared about me. I would've gravitated toward people who had compassion for people like my brother and me. But, instead, I was drawn to kids who were lost and hollow inside, too. *Like attracts like.*

When I became an adult, many of my relatives tried to help me heal by reminding me that I was a child when all these crazy things happened. I don't know whether it's because I was always expected to be an adult or because I reached maturity the way I did, but at some point, I realized something very important: we all have our own pain. This truth has helped me to see everything through the lens of compassion and empathy. It's the reason I believe we should, at some point or another in our journey, all share our stories.

As an adult, I have felt enormous amounts of pain and pleasure. Sometimes when we reach a point of awareness, the pain becomes greater.

I still deal with the pain of my past. But, I know now that we are all human beings with our own tragedies. This allows me to put things in perspective.

Chapter

13

AT OUR MOTHER'S HOUSE, I was given a bed in my sister's room. She had a picture of Kirk Cameron on her wall. She had a crush on him or something like that. She was only eleven at the time.

One day, I tore the picture off the wall in an angry eruption of jealousy. Imagine, I had invaded her space. She didn't even know I was coming. She'd never even met me. She was nine months old when my parents separated.

The scary thing was that I wasn't conscious of what was happening. She had all the things I missed out on as a kid. I wanted to destroy everything she loved.

One day, my sister was putting on Lee Press-On nails. (Mind you, this was the '80s when kids glued plastic nails onto our natural nails and called it fashionable.) I got so angry that I tore the box from her hand and threw them to the ground. Why did she get to have press-on nails and I didn't?

I never, ever had anything against her personally. It was just that she seemed so serene and *in place*. She was so comfortable in her own skin and in the world that surrounded her. She had a lean, athletic body. She had the most fabulous, blonde hair. She pranced around with confidence. In this world I knew nothing about, she fit in. She swam in the pool with her friends. *Friends? What were friends? What did it mean to have a friend?* Sure, she was my sister biologically, but she was a stranger. Then again, so was everyone. I was "acting out" to stress my chaotic emotional state. I had no other way of expressing that I needed help. But I'm not sure I would've gotten any even if I'd flat-out asked.

We were taught that America was a Whore. She was defiled, corrupted, filled with the blood of the saints, murderous, and doomed to hellfire. She would be crushed for the murder of the saints during the End of the World, when the Apocalypse would come and take the saints and bury the Whore with her blood and her sins.

The Bible talks about Babylon the Great, the Mother of Harlots and Abominations of the Earth in Revelation 17:5. Babylon represented everything that went against God. Moses David took this to be a depiction of America. America was Babylon. She—America—would be destroyed by the wrath of God at the end of the world.

Both my brother and I were the embodiments of everything we were taught. The C.O.G. memories and indoctrinations lived deep within our psyche. We tried to suppress their philosophy but we couldn't. We tried to erase it but their belief system was all we knew. We were tortured by it. It prevented us from seeing the world—especially America—as a beautiful place, one where we could find our will, be creative, discover our potential, and prosper as adults.

These ideals became triggers that set us off, destroying every new experience.

I would try to make sense of something wonderful and amazing in this new world, like my sister's innate happiness, her general attitude, and her distinct sense of self. But, somehow, someway, I'd revert to what I was initially taught: that all these people were of *the system* and they were puppets for the Great Whore, the Beast, and the Beast was evil.

· · ·

In my early teens, back in the cult, I was drawn to idols in the outside world. I saw them on posters everywhere. I listened to their music on the bus and on the streets of South America. Their songs echoed of a place I'd never experienced or could even imagine. They spoke of emotions of which I didn't understand. And freedoms that were foreign. These artists were the voices of the outside world.

I remember looking at a poster of Madonna. She was the epitome of cool, that I could tell. But, I feared for myself, for my safety, because I loved her so much. I was secretly afraid that she was evil, and that because I was drawn to her, I was evil, too. She was "of the world." Did that mean if I idolized her that I was, too?

The extreme binaries that were proposed to us were total absolutes of black vs. white. The C.O.G. was It and "the world" was not It. So, everything outside the confines of the organization was lumped together as wrong. And, as mentioned previously, according to their interpretations of the Bible, "the world" was run and owned by the Devil, and so everything in it was of the Devil and would one day be destroyed by the wrath of God. It breaks my heart still when I think about their extremism. Everything that felt beautiful from the outside world was wrong and evil. So, how could I make sense of something I was drawn to that existed out there? It seems so clear to me now: I was being set up to lose if I left, and that's exactly what happened.

Our sister, at eleven, was roughly the same age as my brother and I when we had our first sexual experiences. She was a child. This truth was unfathomable to me, even then. My sister's biggest concerns before we moved in were swim lessons, sleepovers with friends, press-on nails, and such. Then, instantly, she had a front-row seat to her two older siblings suffering from PTSD. We lashed out daily, crying for help and receiving none. Her childhood changed dramatically because of us. Our mother—*her mother*—changed, too.

To make the situation more complicated, my mother and our stepdad had just had a baby. The baby didn't so much concern us, and she was just a half-sister. I knew that my other sister was my full flesh and blood; this added salt to the wounds. She was the target of my envy and obsession.

I didn't feel love for my full sister until much, much later. I only felt a deep and penetrating resentment. Why did she get to live the good life? Why were my brother and I so cursed? Why were we not chosen? How would we ever fit in? How could we ever compete with the beauty and innocence of our sister? We were damaged. We were disgusting. No one had bothered to love us like my sister had been loved. How could we ever manage our lives? And we were so lonely. It's not a word I would normally use to describe my childhood, but if loneliness were a disease, we were in the end stages of it by the time we got to our mother.

My brother didn't bother with our sister too much. His target was the other boys at school. His erratic behavior resulted in suspension and expulsion over and over.

Worse, it seemed that my coming to live with our mother was a trigger for my brother. Here, he had gotten the escape he was looking for, and then there I was. There would always be a dark shadow there to remind him of the cult—that shadow was me. He could never escape, not really.

At the tail end of 1989, he got into one of his worst fights ever. He came home one day with bruised eyes and a broken wrist. After dressing all his wounds with bandages, he looked like he was home fresh from a war. We were always told that we were soldiers against the world (the system). The Bible and Berg (Mo) were our commanders in chief, and we were nothing more than weapons. We fought against everything that did not align with their vision and purpose—against the system. Can you imagine anything more effective than using children to fight your war? It was diabolical. Then, those same children hopped the fence and switched sides one day, from ally to enemy. Children. There were to be no winners in this war. Instead, we internalized this conflict, which triggered a war inside.

Our post-traumatic stress was triggered by every new experience in the "real world" and they were everywhere. Sitting in a classroom; eating dinner with a family we did not know; not having daily indoctrinations projected into our brains; not having routine examinations of our thoughts and evaluations of our actions; not being told who to worship, how to think, what to wear, when to speak, when to eat, when to sleep; not being reminded we were sinners…. No one in my new world, America the Whore, reminded me about praying for my impending doom. Why not? Why was everyone so casual, so different, and so disconnected from my indoctrination—from everything I knew?

Our stepdad tried to be a good role model, to be a fine and good husband for our mom and a loving dad for us. My brother and I had been very transparent from the day we walked into their home about everything: the spankings, the molestation, the creepy brainwashing. Our mom knew it was true. She had expected that much. She had been there herself many moons before we arrived.

My stepdad tried to use a heavy hand with my brother, to create order amid chaos. He'd imagined that's what my brother was used to. In his mind, my brother would submit and obey, listen, be respectful, and understand. That only hardened my brother's heart more.

One day, a few years after I'd arrived, around 1990, I escaped in the night through my bedroom window to meet my friends. When I snuck back in, my stepdad was standing at the bottom of the staircase in his pajamas. He was so sad. Frustrated. Angry. I think I was high on LSD because in my memory he was glowing, like a sad angel. He had a beautiful aura all around him. But, his eyes were so strange. Perplexed. Tormented.

As he stood there, I studied the devastation within them. It was a unique brokenness, like nothing I had ever seen. I could see that he was conflicted and confused and felt helpless, too.

I felt his pain, and I said, "I wish I could be just like you. But I can't." It was hard to recognize that. I would never be as good or as normal as he was. I would never look at another person and wish I could save them or hope that they would accept my love. I couldn't imagine trying to heal another person from all their hurts. No one had held or healed me.

I saw in him a father I'd never had. I saw his love for a mother whose womb I did not remember. All his pain, there it was. He wasn't afraid to show me that he was lost and confused, even though he was the adult in the home. I felt like a parasite feeding on a host of goodness that I would never know as mine.

My life was too complicated. It had never even felt like a life. It was a non-life, absent of me, of my true self, belonging to no one.

Once I spoke the only truth I knew, my stepdad turned and walked upstairs to his room, saying nothing. I walked to my room downstairs, wondering if I would ever know myself or live to speak a new truth, a brighter one that I could call my own.

One time, I got ahold of a six-pack of the cheapest, shittiest beer on the planet. I didn't get it because I enjoyed the taste of piss-water; I was trying to get drunk so I could kill myself. I had found some information from one of my sinister friends that said to kill yourself correctly you had to slice your wrist along the vein, not across the wrist, in order to bleed out. I figured getting really drunk would give me confidence and ease the pain of cutting into my skin. Well, I didn't have a scalpel, so I decided to use a razor. No matter how hard I tried, I could not cut deep enough.

The next morning, I woke up with my wrist bandaged in some kind of gauze and immersed in a bucket of water. I imagine it was supposed to stop the bleeding. To this day, I have no idea who wrapped my arm and got the bucket. It might've been me. It might've been my mother. I honestly don't know.

It was kind of pathetic, honestly. I was sixteen, drinking and doing drugs while living at home and I'd just tried to kill myself—and no one seemed to notice. It was situations like that that made me realize no one was going to rescue me. I was doomed to fail at everything, including dying. So, what was the point of giving a damn? Life had evaded me and even death wasn't interested.

Chapter

14

WHEN I WAS A SOPHOMORE in high school—actually it might have been fall of my junior year—I made friends with a girl that hung with a dark crowd. Her father was a Hell's Angel, or so she'd said. She invited me over to her house. There were tweakers hanging out, drugging themselves to death. It was a real mess and I wondered what the hell I was doing there in the first place. But, there was something seductive about not giving a damn and wandering. I had no apparent way of defending myself against predators (that was obvious). Plus, I'd been victimized over and over for as long as I could remember, which begs the question: How does one defend themselves when they're willing to do whatever, ingest whatever, witness whatever?

This young girl introduced me to cocaine. I remember doing a line, but I couldn't remember much else until I ended up at home in my bed. I felt like shit. It was the worst. I couldn't think. I could barely breathe. I couldn't sleep. All I could do was sit and let my clogged mind wander into oblivion. When I was on cocaine, I was even more numb than usual. It wasn't a happy, confident high for me, like others had claimed. It made me feel sick. Paralyzed. Powerless.

Eventually, my experimentation with drugs dug its talons deep into my heart and broken soul. It was around this time that I became an atheist. If there was a god, I didn't give a damn about him or her or whatever the hell it was. I just didn't care anymore. It seemed that whoever created me was either dead or sleeping by this point.

They didn't give a damn, so why should I?

Chapter

15

I LOOKED IN THE MIRROR and saw a shell of girl. Then I looked into her eyes. Maybe I did a shoddy job on my wrist because my animal instinct was telling me to survive...? I was self-destructing in every way, but death did not come. I couldn't help but wonder: *Why do I exist?*

Shortly after turning sixteen, I landed a job. One day when I was walking to work, this older guy in a red convertible pulled over and asked me if I wanted a ride. He ended up taking me to his house. He proposed a modeling job. All I had to do was let him take some pictures. Once I agreed, he asked if he could tie me up because he wanted to see how I could act, like an actress would in a movie.

He tied me up and began to videotape me. I cried and pleaded with him to let me go. I got lucky. I have always said that I know I have guardians watching over me. He even drove me around the corner from my home and dropped me off.

Knowing my address, he sent me a *Jesus Loves You* card. When I got that in the mail, I felt sick to my stomach. The "real world" just got a little too close to home.

Chapter

16

AROUND 1991, MY BROTHER GOT his first car. In a fair world, I would've gotten my own car first; I was the oldest. My new family never taught us how to drive, so I imagine my brother figured it all out on his own and beat me to this new freedom. I was so jealous. He was independent. It was like having his own car meant that he'd finally made it.

One afternoon, I was walking down the road from our house in California to work at a gas station up the street. I was miserable. Adding insult to injury, my brother pulled over and offered to give me a ride to work. Maybe he pitied me, or maybe he just wanted to show off.

When I got into his car, I completely freaked out and started screaming. I was so angry, tired, and exhausted from feeling so lost. He pulled over and told me to get out. I wanted him to be my knight in shining armor. I wanted him to see and hear my pain. To rescue me. How could he? He couldn't even rescue himself. Just once, I wanted him to be my brother. I needed a role model, someone I could trust, someone who understood me.

In addition to being very good looking with his blue-green eyes and wavy, blond hair, my brother seemed to have things a little bit more together than I did. He was offered modeling jobs. There was an agency that wanted him to act on one of the sitcom shows—they represented people that produced it. Of course, as proclaimed by Moses David, all backsliders would perish in the arms of the Beast. He had a one-way ticket to a self-fulfilling prophecy, which didn't allow him to model for income and be admired for his beauty.

My brother and I grew apart during the years we lived with our mother. We never talked about what had happened in the organization. Our hormones were out of control, too. We had already experimented sexually, and we had mixed feelings about each other on top of everything else. It was a combination of different types of love that manifested in a desire to control one another because we were both too headstrong to give the other any power. Hatred was the result—jealousy, self-hatred, and hatred of each other.

Our mother was desperate for control. At one point, she tried counseling. But, after my first session, my mother told me that I had said to her that I didn't need it and wouldn't cooperate, so she gave up completely. I do remember thinking that the idea of talking to a stranger about things I couldn't even comprehend was ludicrous. Deep down, I didn't want to get my father in trouble or hurt the organization I grew up in—or worse, cause myself so much shame and embarrassment that I would lose the home I was in now. How could I trust these strangers? How could I trust this psychologist? How could I trust anyone? In my experience, all adults were the enemy.

The organization I was born into warned us about therapy. They told us that our enemies would deprogram us, fill us with lies, and take our faith and our right to exist away from "this" organization that was created with God's will in mind. The C.O.G said therapists would force us to worship the Beast. They told us if we were to ever seek one out, we would be prey to the world and all that it had in store for us.

I have asked myself why our mom didn't make weekly therapy mandatory by threatening the roof over our heads, especially since she must've seen my brother and me falling apart by the minute. I imagine that if she had made us go, it would've helped, even though it seemed like nothing short of a miracle could do that.

Because our mom couldn't control the situation or my brother, she shoved Michael into the foster care system. I came home one day and he was gone. He'd been kicked out of several schools by that point. It didn't take long before he ran away from his foster parents.

Next, my mother sent him back to my father and the cult. My aunt, her sister, was appalled by this. She wanted to save him. She took him in. But, that didn't last long. I'm not sure what happened, but he ended up becoming a street kid.

The same thing happened to me one year later. I was finishing up my junior year. Our mother wanted to send me back to the organization. My aunt did the same thing. She and my uncle lived in Kansas. They took me in. They were kind and patient, and it was paradise. Thankfully, I recognized that, even back then.

Although I was grateful and recognized I was in a safe and loving environment, I didn't quite understand why they were being kind to me. What did they want? Would their patience expire? Surely, it would. Living in peace wasn't a thing that a girl like me knew. I was waiting for the other shoe to drop. I imagine it had been the same for my brother. We'd never had normalcy or experienced unconditional love or kindness just for the sake of it.

The organization and our father had told us that they loved us, but where were they now? What was the meaning of the word love, anyway? There were no true feelings or actions to back it up in the cult.

I suppose we both tried to love these people back: our mother, sister, stepdad, and my aunt and uncle. But, what was love? It always felt so conditional and abstract. We knew nothing of normal, parental love; we couldn't recognize it. I couldn't even tell you now if she had tried to love us normally. It would be years before I would allow myself to accept love.

Chapter

17

AFTER I GRADUATED HIGH SCHOOL at my aunt's in June of 1992, I was sent back to California to live with my mom and stepdad again. That was the beginning of my six-year "death walk."

My parents had made it clear that because I was eighteen, my time there would be temporary. I needed to find my own place and my own path. They would no longer help me. They had done the best they could and now it was time to move on. They had lives that needed to be lived, and the burdens that we bore were more than they could handle. In their minds, they'd fulfilled their duty.

Had they? Was releasing me from their care simply another item being checked off their list? Or, was I being set free because I was a daily reflection of her failure as a mother? She had two more children to raise. I imagine seeing me around made that more challenging. But, anyone with eyes would've known I was neither emotionally ready nor physically capable of making it alone in the real world.

By that point, the only emotion in my system I could register was shame. I was raised and brainwashed to feel nothing but shame for being a sinner. Now, I was free to love, but I was never asked: "Do you understand what love is?" As for going out and finding my destiny, I didn't know what I wanted to do with my "self," my free will, or my power. I was not the me I am today. I was not Marie.

When I lived with my aunt and uncle, I tasted goodness and experienced maternal and paternal love for the very first time. I began to understand the concept of friendship, if only on the surface. I wasn't with them long enough to erase fourteen years of brainwashing and abuse, but if it weren't for my senior year with them, I would've never graduated high school.

• • •

Back in California, I found all my old high school friends and the trouble began. I couldn't keep a job. I wrecked my first car. It didn't take long before I ended up living with boyfriends. I hopped from house to house, person to person. My druggie friends liked me enough to get me high for free.

I somehow managed to find a steady boyfriend. He was very sweet and cute. He was a drummer. I think he loved me, but I still didn't know what love meant. All I knew was I liked him and he was nice in return. I remember thinking how bizarre it was, that after all the meaningless sex I'd had, I'd found a boyfriend who loved me. I was hopeful that I could be faithful and love him in return. But, I was so disconnected from myself. The path I saw in front of me was eroded and unstable. The real Marie was still only an apparition in my heart. I could not love. Couldn't even begin to imagine how the mechanics of real love worked.

My boyfriend did hard drugs. He would feed them to me for breakfast, lunch, and dinner. But, as time passed, the excitement, the newness of our relationship, faded. Then, situations started separating us. I found myself wandering again, like a gypsy moving from house to house. There was no fidelity or loyalty to my boyfriend. There was only a dream-like death walk. It surrounded me, day and night.

My life as a street kid progressed heavily around this time. My boyfriend would go to Los Angeles and play at this tweaker's studio, and when we'd cross paths, I'd go along. The outside of the studio was painted a dismal, rusty red. Inside, the walls were all black. The place was always filled with smoke and sweat and drugs. All these hardcore junkies would let me get high and I would watch them jam. I lived in a "kind of crazy" like you wouldn't believe. I was a walking corpse, a shell dragging around a dying soul. One day, my drummer boyfriend left me there after a gig and never returned.

At some point during my delirium, I found a new "boyfriend" who let me live in his house. He would get me high, then he'd leave me there for days on end. I had no food, nothing but the clothes on my back and a few items in a tiny suitcase. Soon enough, he got sick of me and kicked me out.

During those days on the streets, I would walk for hours. I had no destination in mind, no life to live. I searched for other lost souls. I wanted someone to find me, pick me up, and take me home. But, none of the people I found had a home. When I looked into their eyes, it was like our souls recognized each other's—the nothingness of being. We weren't living so much as existing.

After three years of being a street kid in Los Angeles, I didn't recognize myself in the mirror anymore. The lovely, lost, lonely girl I used to know was long gone. I didn't even look human. I was sickly skinny and all my beauty had faded. I'm surprised I didn't scream at the horror of my own reflection. Too tired, I guess.

· · ·

I'd been wandering the streets of Venice Beach for days, maybe weeks, when I found a lady…or she found me.

She took me in. Her apartment was low-income with a strong scent of mold. She had clothes strewn all around like she'd been hoarding them for years.

I crawled up on a pile of clothes in a corner of her living room, hoping to blend in. I only came out of hiding when I thought someone had arrived with more drugs.

One day, a man came over. I was hiding behind the mountain of filthy laundry, or so I thought. He took off his clothes and laid down, sinking in his own oblivion, a demon eyeing his prey. The lady told me I could have all the drugs I wanted. All I had to do was please the demon. By that time, all my womanhood had fled. The Children of God disciple that had danced naked for attention and tempted adult men to have sex with her was dead. The sight of this man petrified me. It brought back memories of times when I thought sex would heal me.

I turned to the lady and shook my head. She became so angry. No one was getting drugs if I didn't please him. She kicked me out like a wet rat into the crumbling world.

I wandered around Venice Beach for a few more months—time had little relevance to me. I would stare at the ocean longingly, begging for it to take me home. It was so beautiful, and I was nothing. Even the ocean didn't want me enough to swallow me up. I felt like I would never belong to anything.

I ended up walking straight onto a freeway divider. I stood in the middle of the intersection and waited. The police came and picked me up. They took me to their station and asked me what my name was. I could not remember. They asked me what date it was. I did not know. They asked me who the president was. I did not know. I heard one officer say, "She thinks she's in a movie." I remembered movies. My memory logged my life like a movie, frame by frame—but it was jarring, loud, and the colors were so dark, like watching a horror film. Jesus being crucified on the cross—ten times, one hundred times, one million times—that was the movie I knew best.

They saw that I was sick. They recognized that I wasn't a threat to them, so they took me to a mental hospital. In the hospital, they drugged the death out of me. Regardless, there was nothing they could do. I existed in a place that was not real. I did not have the blessing of knowing myself, which would have given me a destination upon which I could return. I imagine someone who becomes an alcoholic or has a nervous breakdown remembers a time when life was okay or at least bearable. I had no point of reference. I was a crippled body that housed a crippled soul. I was told by one of the nurses that it was 1996. That's when it hit me that I'd been on the streets for almost four years.

One day, they released me to a group home for the mentally ill, telling my mother it was for the best, as I would never live a normal life.

What did they ever really know about me?

Chapter

18

I CAN'T REMEMBER EXACTLY HOW long I was sedated in the hospital, but it was 1997 when I moved into the group home.

I wasn't there for long before I ran away.

I met a young man at a rave in California. He said he fell in love with me the moment he saw me, which was quite ridiculous. But, as starving as I was for affection, I believed him.

We ran away to San Francisco. It didn't take long for him to recognize that there was something wrong with me. Holding a conversation was still challenging, and the idea of living a normal life was something I couldn't imagine.

He ended up asking me to leave his home, so I ended up on the streets of San Francisco, searching for something that I didn't believe I'd ever find.

I was so disillusioned with my life, disconnected from the Divine. I was starving—physically, spiritually, emotionally. My heart was so broken from being abandoned by everyone that had ever claimed to love me. Even those who didn't love me, but somehow played a big part in my life, couldn't manage to stick around.

Then, out of the blue one night, I ran into my brother. We met randomly at a convenience store. He was living on the streets, too. Did we meet by chance? Was it destiny?

There we were, face to face. It was dark—way past midnight— but I would've recognized him anywhere. He didn't look anything like the beautiful, blond boy I knew, so hip, so cool.

His hair was long and brown. It rested curly around his shoulders. He wore traveling clothes, looking more like a hippie than a ladies' man. He gave me his pager number and told me to call him the next day.

I did.

We met by a train. We sat down, chatted. He bought me a vegan burrito, said I looked like I was starving. I probably hadn't eaten in days. I remember what he told me that day more vividly than any other memory from our entire lives together. I had on a short-sleeved shirt and he could see the track marks all over my arms.

"Stop it," he said, studying my arms. But, what he really meant was, "Please stop hurting yourself because I love you and I don't want to see you suffer like this."

Our little sister had watched him mainline one day in a closet at home, so he understood the pain I was in. He seemed to be drug-free that day. Honestly, I'll never know for sure.

That was the last conversation I'd ever have with Michael. After we sat for a few minutes, he said he needed to leave. Then he was gone.

Knowing that Michael cared about my wellbeing gave me a sliver of hope. He was right; using purely chemical drugs like heroin, meth, and cocaine were so unbelievably harmful. When I mainlined, the unnatural effect was greater than anything I'd ever experienced. First of all, it was a direct violation of my temple: the temple of my body. In order to mainline, you violate your arms, legs, hands, and any other area where you can find a vein. You pierce your skin only to inject it with pure death.

I have never heard of a human overdosing on marijuana, a natural remedy that grows from the earth, but people overdose on hard, man-made drugs every day. Once my veins were filled with poison, it felt like I was leaving my body and entering a world of total chaos. At first, the feeling was indescribable relief, but then the drug takes over and you have no control. Doing drugs was a form of entrapment, except, unlike with the cult, I was doing it to myself.

I remember looking at my arms after Michael left me sitting on the concrete pavement by the train. It was horrifying. It was like I had leprosy or some other kind of disease. I was a perpetual victim because I was too out of control to defend myself. I only had enough life in me to carry my poisoned body from one chaotic situation to another.

When I reached my mid-twenties, around 1998, I was so sick at heart. I was so tired. I longed for something bigger to give my life meaning. Something bigger than my past. N.A. and A.A. never worked. I didn't feel like I belonged there. I felt that their code was built on limited thinking, not on awareness and transcendence. Even A.A. seemed to be for more normal addicts than me.

Chapter

19

ONE DAY I WAS LYING on the floor, staring at a ceiling, thinking about the organization I'd grown up in. I vaguely remembered a sense of peace that I was famished for. It was like there was an inner light that still burned in my soul. I lay there thinking even if I had my will and my choices taken away from me, at least I had food to eat and would be surrounded by family.

I can't recall exactly how this happened or why I remember the date, but it was December 17, 1998 when I got up from that floor, did some research, and found a C.O.G. home right in the city.

I know this might sound crazy, but that day it felt like my inner light, my internal guidance system, wanted me to return to the only home I'd ever known. Given my circumstances, all I could think was that it would be better than what I had. It would be better than nothing.

Now I recognize that moment of clarity as so much more. That was the day I opened my heart to the Divine for the first time. I was sick of failing at everything in life, including dying. This step, as obscure as it may sound, was propelled by survival instinct. It was my right, after all, to survive. I wanted the opportunity. I was worthy of it, at least that's what I heard the Divine whisper. I am only beginning to fully grasp the impact of that insight and the action it generated as I write this book in my forties.

Seeing this truth allows me to understand that the Divine essence will use anything and everything to reach out to those in need. The Divine will use the strangest, most unexpected and unorthodox means to aid any human soul to find their own eternal flame—their inner light. This lesson has been essential in my healing process.

• • •

Coming full circle, I returned to what I knew. The C.O.G. was kind enough to take me in. I thought of myself as a prodigal daughter. Being with them was a breath of fresh air in comparison to the hard life on the streets. The second time around, the lure of their ideologies made perfect sense to me. I could see why so many disillusioned young people fell for it. After breathing in the smog from the cruel world, they were looking for the same fresh air I was.

Even though my mother left the organization after four years, my father had found his home with these people. He had found a sanctuary. He was able to be a free-spirited hippie, and, at the same time, he was no longer a lost druggie. Seeing the C.O.G. through adult eyes, through their eyes, would end up playing a vital role in my recovery.

Of course, after living with the C.O.G. again for about six months, I realized that the story was familiar, and not for me. There was this young girl who they called a new disciple. She changed her legal name, as they often did. Changing your name meant that you were a new creature in Christ. There was another new disciple, a young man who had changed his name, as well.

Once these new disciples had hit the six-month mark, they were given the rights to share their bodies with other members. (They were both over the age of eighteen.) An older man, who had been in the group for many, many years, consistently reached out to the young girl to ask her to share with him sexually. She had told him multiple times that she did not feel comfortable partaking in that experience. He kept on telling her that if she wanted to be involved in the organization, she would need to open herself up. Be more revolutionary. This meant that she should be unselfish and share her body with him.

In her eyes, that was sexual assault. She became so appalled with his consistent and annoying pursuit, she left the home. Right before she left, she confided in me. She wanted me to know why she was leaving. Not long after her departure, the young man left, too.

I was next. I was not conforming the way they'd hoped. I also needed some medicine and treatment for severe post-traumatic stress disorder, but I didn't want any medicine. I was trying to be radical and trust Jesus to heal me. That was causing me even more stress.

I found out years later that certain mental health issues are derivative of mounting stressors that occur (especially) in early childhood. This is one of the main causes of post-traumatic stress disorder.

I wanted to show the organization how desperate I was to forget. They had given me food, clothing, and shelter. But, I felt overwhelmed to be back in familiar territory. This was the same territory that had caused the original post-traumatic stress. I also started facing the same situations with the same sexual elements.

I was reminded that sexual harassment and manipulation, in one form or another, was a part of who they were. Even swingers in the real world adhere to rules: if you ask and someone says "no," then that should be respected. Using guilt or shame or God as a tactic to get someone into bed is harassment; it's cruel and it's illegal.

Somewhere along the line, I must've called my mom to let her know I was in the C.O.G. again. In spite of her anathema for that organization, she came to visit. She wanted to be close to me, to see if I was okay. I felt like I was living in some kind of distorted reality, given that she was nowhere to be found when I was homeless.

I sometimes ask myself why she didn't rescue me. After much studying, learning, and researching, I recognize that many parents have children before they are ready. They are ill-equipped and without the education and resources needed to provide the proper support.

With my mother, it was more than that. True, she had not been ready to have children. She didn't have her own life stabilized. But, she relived her own pain every time she saw my brother and me. She relived losing us—feeling helpless like she had no control over where we were or what we had become. On top of that, we'd come back to her in more pieces. And, like my father, she was only human.

I understand this truth. It is not an excuse for her neglect, but I understand that my brother and I were so damaged, we had so much going on, and we were so hard to handle, that resolution seemed impossible. Our father didn't try to rescue us, either, but the situation he was in was complicated and difficult. There was so little room for a way out. He would have been deemed a backslider as well, and his own religion and convictions kept him controlled and at bay.

My brother and I were collateral damage of a bad decision and a relationship gone wrong. The fact that our mother had the courage to come back to the place that had caused her so much pain and disorientation was surreal and comforting. I can only imagine what was going through her mind that day. Maybe when she'd heard my voice, I sounded okay for the first time. Maybe she, too, heard the voice of the Divine and came to see me.

I appreciated the strangers at the C.O.G. They were once family and acted as such by taking me back in. Even though I had backslid and left the organization, I had returned—humbled by my own foolishness, my own pride. It was like I was there to tell them, "You were right. Leaving was wrong. See? I paid the price for it—just like you said." My self-fulfilling prophecy had come full circle in a demented yet ironic way. The naked truth, ego aside, is that familiarity possesses great power and influence over our decisions.

It was my choice to return, and I'm grateful for the takeaway. I was given an opportunity to understand their good intentions, and, for the first time in my life, I understood my father and mother—their motivation for joining and subscribing to the cult's truth.

Buddhism teaches a very important concept about detachment. When we are able to observe and postpone judgment, we have arrived at a place of awareness where we can evolve with more understanding, compassion, empathy, and love. Because I am self-aware now, I recognize I went back to the organization to rest and recover in the safety of familiar arms.

After that phase passed, the sinking feeling that doom was right around the corner surfaced. I was reminded that the cult was not built on light and love and innocence; a demon was lurking. That demon would remind me the End of the World was near. Believing this, staying put, adhering to their doctrines and lifestyle, was the price I would pay for existing in that space with them.

This distortion of peace was not real. It never had been. It never would be. I didn't know what exactly I believed in, but I knew that was not it.

In the spring of 1999, I had been off my medicine for many months. I was tired and weary. I think my mannerisms and my spirit must have been frightening the other members of the home. One day, while I lay in my bed, the leaders gathered outside my room and prayed to Jesus to cast out my demons. I tried to ignore their voices, praying so loudly on the other side of the door. It reminded me of why I would never be a disciple.

Thank goodness it had that effect because, after a few minutes, they came into my room and told me to leave. I was the black sheep, the heathen goat, the stubborn, willful one, the child with her own inner strength. I was not a clone. I was not going to yield if it did not resonate. I was not going to bow to whatever they deemed to be true. I was divergent. I was different, and that was not acceptable.

Chapter

20

BECAUSE OF MY OWN SPIRITUAL awakening, after having risen above so much chaos and confusion—and after many years of therapy and education—I am reminded that my purpose in life is not about revenge. I wish no ill will on anyone in that organization. Their attempt to deny the laws of man and find original innocence in a commune lifestyle is brave and commendable—in some ways.

I don't have terrible memories of all those people, either. I have some great ones. We didn't have to think about school or work. We were sheltered from the outside. This provided me with a momentary grace that I still think of fondly.

But, the darkness I felt inside me as I matured spread like wildfire, especially when I began to ask *why* questions and think for myself. I began to hear and see the world outside of the confines of that organization, and I began to hunger for that freedom.

Chapter

21

WHEN I LEFT THE C.O.G. home in California, it was in the fall of 1999. I tried church. I thought maybe there was some redemption for me there. I ended up living with a youth group—they were Christian girls who were on a mission to save lost souls. They'd dedicated one or two years of service to help others.

Once again, I was that ragged, cute, kitten in the rain, just waiting for someone to pick me up and take me home—for better or for worse.

What they were to me, at that time, was nothing short of angelic. They appeared like an apparitional miracle. They took me in. They fed me. They told me that God loved me. They showed me a different version of the cult I was born into. They prayed with me. They prayed for me. They gave me an idea of love that was filled with so much caring. In a way, it was a pure version of love that I'd never experienced. It reminded me of the life I'd had as a child. But, they were different from the C.O.G. They encouraged me to go to college.

As long as I went to church on Sunday and I didn't dress provocatively, then I could go to school and they would feed me, love me, and pray for me.

I was lucky. Because I was so poor, the community college allowed me to go to school for free; I received a grant from the government. I began to see the magic of an organized and productive life. I was going to school, I was doing well, and during the time I stayed with the mission group, I was drug-free. It was the year 2000. I was twenty-six.

One day, they told me about a baptism class. It was a purification ritual. The purpose was to allow me the opportunity to be cleansed. Symbolically, I would walk into the water and all of my past would be washed away. I would be officially redeemed.

I remember going through that class material and all I could think about was what I would wear for the ritual, and how elated I was to return to the ocean—the same one I was hoping would swallow me whole would now bring me back to life. All the students would get baptized by God via the ocean.

Even though in their eyes it was a Christian ritual and bound by certain old-fashioned philosophies, to me it was something very different. At that time, I was following their biblical ritual, but today I recognize that what happened was a very powerful thing. Even though I did not recognize the symbolic nature of what I went through, I was grateful. The water symbolized the Womb of Creation. The "womb" took me into her arms and washed me clean of the past. And I returned home—back into her safety and familiarity, so I could be reborn.

The clothes I chose to wear included a white shirt and a pair of white pants. The lady of the house told me that I couldn't wear them; they were too see-through. I responded by putting on another white shirt, and we called it a day.

Regardless, divergence still coursed through my veins. I loved the mission girls for caring. I appreciated them for bringing me a sliver of sunshine in a dark world. But, my inner instincts remained nonconformist.

I met a girl that I was attracted to. She was born on the exact same day as I was. I thought of her as my twin. I soon found out that she liked girls, too. I immediately grew fond of her and we became romantically involved.

One day, I brought her home to the group. We went into my bedroom to do homework. Truthfully, we were there to linger with each other. We wanted to feel the impulse of our bodies lying next to one another's on the bed. Our intimate attraction soon became transparent to the others. This, among other things, was deemed inappropriate. According to a few scriptures, specifically in the King James Version, it is said that homosexuals will not be eligible to inherit God's world. I find that statement to be cruel, judgmental, and lacking in any kind of human love or compassion for our nature as human beings and who we are authentically. It makes me sick to know that people have been so discriminated against because of who they are. (For a reference, please see Revelations 22:15, 1 Corinthians 6:9,10 and Galatians 5:19–21…among others.)

That same semester, I signed up for a yoga class. I had to practice. That was my homework. I decided to practice my yoga poses in the living room of the house. One of the girls saw me and asked me to stop. She said that yoga was a symbol of worshiping the Egyptian Sun God, Ra. Honestly, even if it was, I would not have had a problem with that. I find yoga to be liberating, an amazing form of meditation and relaxation. I know about the goddesses, their powers and symbolic nature. Being a woman who is repressed by a patriarchal society, I feel irrevocably connected to them. But, at that time, I only felt heartbroken. I was being judged for something so wonderful and so innocent.

These things that I loved were forbidden. I felt the shame once again, backdropping against the innocence of my life. Yet, in my mind, I was doing nothing wrong.

To top it off, the Mormon boys at my college would come up to me in their clean suits, religious doctrines in hand. They gave me one of their copies and I brought that book home. In my naivety, I showed it to one of the girls. That was a no-no. The Mormons were a cult. They were dangerous and deceitful.

I was simply exploring my faith. Trying so desperately to assert myself. To find my identity that had been muffled and clogged in my dark soul for so long. I did find some inner peace living with these girls, but when push came to shove, it was all about control. So, my stay with them didn't last more than six months.

This group helped me to get back on my feet. College was something I never imagined I would or could do. I met all kinds of amazing people there. I was mesmerized by my teachers. I admired their ability to push beyond ignorance—using knowledge.

I still look back on the experience with thoughts of gratitude and grace. These workers were kind. They were honest. In fact, I imagine that I might've never made it out of my dire situation if it weren't for their help. But, as per usual, I was not like them.

That's something most religions can never understand or contend with—exploring one's faith and one's options. Once I became transparent and open, that was the end of the road.

Shortly after, I embarked on a journey to get out of California. I connected with the couple in the C.O.G. that had first taken me in, back in 1998. They were with the organization—the ones I'd stayed with when I first desired a connection with the Divine. I told them I had reformed and needed an escape route. They told me about a mission's home in Oregon.

They said they would take me into their home and help me get on my feet—to start anew. I was so desperate. I didn't want to return to the life I hated so much, but I just couldn't conform to this modern church idea. It was too stifling. I couldn't do yoga. I couldn't be gay. I couldn't bring home the Book of Mormon. I couldn't think or speak for myself. I couldn't explore who I was or find my own identity. I couldn't find my wings.

I packed my bags and moved to Oregon to live with this mission's group. Moving away from California was the best thing I ever did for myself. I thank the Universe for working on my behalf. This mission group's leaders had, at one time, been affiliated with the C.O.G., but they ended up moving on. They were the one exception to the rule when it came to what they were all about. They really cared about me. They really, really loved me. They still do. They're now involved in a Jewish Messianic mission where they teach others about their faith. They think of me on every Sabbath, and they place a piece of bread on their altar of gratitude. These two beautiful souls helped me get back on my feet. I got an apartment. For the first time in my entire life, I was self-sustaining.

I know that I've come full circle multiple times. But, with these people, it was different. Because of them, I believe in miracles. They never had any expectations. They only wanted to see me blossom and thrive. It's people like them who give me faith that there's a

Divinity that surpasses all religion. It's simply pure, unconditional love. That's what anchors me.

After arriving in Oregon, I decided to go to Portland Community College. I wanted to see if I could make my way through school. I had nothing better to do, and I craved independence and productivity.

I roamed from church to church, searching for some kind of solidarity. I looked for something I could wrap my head around. Even though I felt a sense of community in these different places, and I did feel a sort of unity and acceptance, there were still no gay people. And that bothered me. Also, the prosperity doctrine that some churches promoted seemed more about getting people's money than anything else. The crazy things people would say made my stomach turn. For example, one time someone said that the Scottish Masons are in league with the Devil, which is absurd. They see God through architecture, science, and the arts. I know this because when I was in college, I randomly picked up a book about Masonic faith.

Those incidences always brought me back to a convoluted place where an us vs. them mentality existed. Couple that with the underlying concept that we are weak, sinners, broken, and never good enough. And, of course, let's not forget the destruction of the world because we can't get it right or be good enough for God. I felt sad inside because that whole story seemed to be what was broken. Of course, if we lived like it was predicted, we would always be the crippled, dumb, blind sheep that needed someone to remind us that we just can't make it without being codependent upon a God that uses judgment and fear to scare people into submission. Even the concept of grace wasn't pure grace to me. There were always conditions: don't be gay, don't be divergent, don't follow other spiritual paths because they are false religions—the list goes on. The psychology behind the idea of these binaries creates an us vs. them mentality, which can spawn religious violence, discrimination, and a level of superiority—one group over the other. People use this false sense of superiority as a right to damn, doom, or exploit others.

I knew these people were trying to help. They, too, were trying to find solidarity in what they believed. It didn't take long to realize that they were convoluted and distorted as well. I honor the fact that they opened their doors and took me in as a sister. But every time I dove beneath the surface, I found that the deeper message would drown me. That seemed inevitable.

I sought refuge in Buddhist temples. I loved the Nichiren temples. They were modern. They believed that through meditation and chanting your song to the Universe, you could create your own reality based on certain universal principles and guidelines. Buddhists believe that everyone can be a Buddha. They speak about respecting humanity, life, and our sense of self. They believe that in order to awaken and understand the journey of awareness, we must face our light and our shadow. In other words, to understand the potential for light, we must understand the potential for darkness—specifically, to face our own inner demons and conquer them.

Through all of this adventure, I discovered what I didn't like. I discovered that I believed in something much more universal. I wanted to find it, and modern Christian churches didn't have the recipe I was looking for.

In some kind of desperation, I googled "Universal Faith" and found the Unitarian Universalist Church. It was the first church I'd ever found that had gay and lesbian ministers. This made me smile. There were gay couples with their children. *Finally!* I thought. A church that didn't give a damn what your background was or who you were. They only cared about loving one another and being connected to the Divine. They cared about social issues. Black lives matter. Gay rights matter. Transsexual lives matter. Homeless lives matter. My life mattered, divergent as I may be.

I began to see that the powers of the Divine were so much bigger than any one religion, political regime, cult, organization, parent, or friend could define. I even found a Science of Mind Church, which believed that the Divine Presence is already within us. We just have to wake it up inside of ourselves through spiritual practices and awareness. I was no longer being beaten into submission. I was no longer shamed or shunned for my meditation practices, yoga experiences, Buddhist principals, or feminist views.

As I matured into my faith, I studied a lot of feminist and goddess spirituality. Some of it was considered Pagan. I educated myself about absolutely everything. I discovered that Paganism was rooted deep in my heart. Pagans celebrated the goddesses and gods of earth, and cultures like Roman, Egyptian, Greek, Celtic, Brazilian, Hawaiian, African, etc. It was all about the cycles and rhythms of life and death. Each used symbolism to describe the roots of our humanity intertwined with our animal selves. Specifically, the relationship between nature and nurture. Nonetheless, Paganism has been described by many Christians as a heathen way of life.

The difficult part of this truth is that many patriarchal religions describe everything in terms of black and white. There is a scripture in the Bible that says, "You are either for me, or against me" (Matthew 10:20).

Regardless of the original context or meaning, that passage has been interpreted in such a way that either you believe in X, Y, Z, or you are of the world. The world is of the Devil. Therefore, based off this definition, a platform of distinctive binaries produces a line of separation. People who choose to be independent, divergent, homosexual, or otherwise are people who, according to this view, are deemed unworthy because they are shades of gray and rainbow. They refuse to conform to religious ideas that create barriers and incite judgment. It would be nice to imagine that hate and fear were on one side, and love and coexistence were on the other. Instead, many religions foster hatred and judgment against others. So, the binary becomes: you are either heathen, or you are saved.

In my life now, I do not associate my connection to Paganism with an abstract definition of Satan or an evil representation of a biblical angel, Lucifer. This mythological creature gave the knowledge of good and evil to humanity. According to some Christian interpretations, humanity was deceived by Lucifer. We ate from the forbidden tree only to be cursed by our Creators for eternity. This is the story of the "Fall of Humanity," which can be found in Genesis 3.

After all that I have studied and learned, I have a very different perspective. Even though, to me, this story is a myth, I believe that this angel gave us the knowledge of "good and evil" on purpose, and that our Creators were very much aware of this, even allowing it intentionally. Personally, I refer to this dichotomy as a gift of light and shadow. This gift was given to humanity to teach us about who we are, to make us stronger, and to help us to learn to navigate life and the world. And, to actualize our full potential.

Chapter

22

I GRADUATED FROM PORTLAND STATE University in 2006 with a bachelor's degree in Language Arts and Education. This was nothing short of Divine—a true miracle combined with a ton of self-will. I landed a position shortly thereafter in my field as an educational coach. Education was my healer. It taught me that I was smart. I had intellect. I had a strong will that could accomplish amazing and wonderful things. I was capable of thinking deeply and loving hard. This I did not know about myself, as I had never been taught to believe in my own potential.

By this time, I'd already moved past so many pieces of my life that were shattered and broken. I found a way to rebuild myself out of dust and ashes. None of my friends knew anything about my past, except that it was rough. I got married. Life became normal. I started living my true life for the first time.

Regardless of this most-welcomed normality I was experiencing, I couldn't help but notice the pain that still throbbed in my being. It was like there was a knife inside my heart and any movement triggered sharp pain. I decided to find a therapist to help me understand why, after so many accomplishments, I still felt so much pain. I was a living, breathing miracle, that I knew; yet, I still existed in the similitude of life's shadow. My heart still ached and begged to understand more of why and how I had gone through so much—and why I made it through.

I worked with a clinical therapist for the next five years. She noticed that I was riddled with guilt. I felt guilty for my divergent faith. I felt guilty about the errors and mistakes I'd made during the time of my rebellion. I felt guilty that I was once an atheist. I felt guilty about loving women as well as men. I felt guilty for my brother's psychological break because of the heavy hand of my father—for my inability to know how to stick up for him. I felt guilty he had died while I survived. I felt guilty when I wasn't successful enough at work. I felt guilty about the struggles I had with the man I married.

One day, my therapist said, "Guilt is a waste of energy. Are you going to change what you did by feeling guilty about it? Is badgering yourself about the past going to solve the problems that you face every day?" The answer was simple: no. So, what was the solution?

I continued to work with this therapist, attending sessions at least once a month, sometimes once a week. I dug deep into my own abyss. I pulled out the dead carcass of my soul and looked at those old bones, brittle and corroded. I learned to see myself in all of my darkness through eyes of compassion, care, and love.

My therapist was intelligent and kind. She made our sessions a place of peace. I knew that working with her was confidential. For the first time in my life, I felt like there was no one in the world that would or could judge me but myself. I felt safe. There was no

Christian there to tell me that my feelings were a result of sin. There was no boss to tell me that my feelings of inadequacy might get me fired. There was no father or mother to ignore me or shun me for my rebellious nature. There was only me, in that place of sanctity and solitude, working one-on-one with my therapist.

When I was done with the most painful part of my inner exploration, I felt brand new. I'd found a sunny horizon in knowing that, somehow, this woman absolved me of all my guilt and shame just by listening to me. I was in a much better place, mentally. After that, I craved a sense of spirituality that was more emotional. I wanted a therapist to breathe life back into my wounded-but-healing soul. I looked around on the internet to see what I could find. I saw a picture of this woman. Her hair was long and blonde. It christened her shoulders like the sweetest sunrise. I felt a warmth radiate from her eyes. They were soft and blue. I gave her a call. I asked for a session. After I revealed my past, she told me that she had been married to a Mormon for years. She understood the cultic prison— their way or the highway. She told me she had divorced him. She had the courage to do so, even though they had children. She understood me like no one else. With her, I was able to explore the full potentiality of my spiritual self.

We did a lot of deprogramming with a therapy technique called EMDR, which is hypnotic training. I would go into those places of deep darkness and fear and challenge myself to find my own place of inner awareness and peace. It's because of my work with her that I learned to see my father, my mother, and the cult through eyes of empathy, compassion, and forgiveness. Even though I was angry and repulsed, I could still search within my soul and try to understand their reasons. Their perspectives. Why they did what they did. Why they were who they were.

My first therapist had asked me years before: "What do you really want?" I thought about that for a long time. Now, I have an answer: What I really want is to understand my years of survival. To see them with enlightened eyes. To forgive. Empathize. Transcend. To tell my story to a world full of people that, too, have muzzles over their mouths. People who are suffocating in silence, thinking that they cannot and should not be brave enough to tell their story.

The only way I can tell my story with confidence is to keep the ultimate goal in mind. My first step is to forgive. I must forgive those who wronged me so that I can forgive my own actions from the past. I must seek to understand. At the same time, I must carry my warrior spirit. My warrior spirit has a black whip of intentions and a sword made of gold. With these weapons, I slay unwanted thoughts, images, ideas, or perspectives. I rid myself of my darkest demons. I exonerate myself and the bitter world of my childhood. In this forgiveness, I find my personal gift: the gift of my will and emancipation.

Chapter

23

I MENTIONED EARLIER THAT I had gotten married. My husband, who was my boyfriend for two years prior, is Latino and very proud of his skin. He desperately wanted me to get pregnant. I told him numerous times before we got married that I didn't want to have biological children. He kept trying to convince me on the grounds that he would never get to see his own flesh in the world. I felt terrible for denying him his dream. The guilt worked its magic, and I decided to try. I got pregnant.

It was a nightmare from day one. I was worried all the time. I lived over an hour away from work and clocked between forty and forty-five hours a week. The daycare we had in our hometown was terrible. I obsessed over logistics like that. Also, I wanted to remain detached while carrying the child because, if the baby didn't make it, I didn't want to suffer. That created guilt: If I didn't become attached, the Universe would think I didn't want my baby. If I didn't become attached, complications would arise. I got off my very strict diet. I gained weight because my doctors told me I needed to eat 2,500 calories a day, which, with my slower metabolism, was insane.

I gave into the fear and guilt. I did genetic testing to ensure the baby was not sick. I was over forty, so complications were a real threat. When all the testing came back normal, we named the baby Jayden Gadiel.

Two weeks after the test results, I stood in the shower feeling overwhelmed. I was worried that we were not going to have the resources to care for our unborn son. I wanted to give him the life we'd never had. Paralyzed by fear, I quoted the biblical verse that Christ uttered before he faced the cross: "Please let this cup pass from me" (Matthew 26:39).

When I went in for my next check-up, the baby had no heartbeat. I knew that I had bargained with the Universe and my prayers had been answered.

I would be lying if I told you that I wasn't heartbroken. I was willing to face potential complications being forty; I was willing to be put on bedrest. My health insurance was dependent on a not-so-secure job, and I was willing to face that—to face everything for the sake of my husband. But, the Universe understood me and my true will and wouldn't let me make that sacrifice, not even for the man I loved.

Ask and you shall receive.

Chapter

24

AROUND THE TIME WHEN I began to write this book, my mother and I grew closer. She confessed that she never should've had my brother or me. I remember hearing the words and feeling relieved. They were so honest. I had always known this truth and hearing her admit it validated me. Under different life circumstance, a daughter would've been hurt or even shattered by that kind of confession, but I knew better. I held her in a place of grace and understanding. She said that she had never been given a choice about childbirth. There was no education on women's rights. The organization I was born into provided her with neither the knowledge nor a choice about whether she would get pregnant.

I believe in free will and personal choice, especially for women whose rights have been repeatedly taken away. My mother did not mean to hurt me; I understand that now. When she bared her truth, it wasn't about me; it was about not being ready to be a mother. She was a mom of three so early in life, by the time she was just twenty-three.

She was going through so much internally. On top of that, she was facing the reality that she'd have to produce more children for the C.O.G without the ability to choose. Their mode of operation was you copulate, you procreate. Choosing when or with whom you had children was not trusting the Lord. "Making love" on demand was being obedient to the first commandment in the Bible: "Be fruitful and multiply" (Genesis 1:28). It was much more romanticized, but that was the message.

In an environment where it's encouraged for women to share their bodies with other members of the organization, there's no telling who they'd be impregnated by. For young teens without a partner, like my brother and me, that meant having babies regardless of who would be there to raise them. In those cases, the children would be raised by the organization.

The United Nations teaches sex education to many countries in the world. Groups like theirs make it a priority to inform women that they have rights—that they do not have to procreate unless they are ready and able to provide for their families. Having children is a huge responsibility and a privilege. Rearing a child is an honor that should not be taken lightly.

So many nations have babies born into poverty. Why? Because women don't know they have a choice. Sometimes it's because they were raped; sometimes other circumstances come into play, like religion. Making a choice about their pregnancy is forbidden. They have babies to the detriment of their own health or that of the baby. That's why I understand my mother's perspective and forgive her. It hurts, yes. But, I understand.

THE GIFT OF WILL

I could relate so well because when I was fourteen, after I left the organization and found myself in a new world, I was petrified of getting pregnant. That feeling did not abandon me when I escaped the C.O.G. Rather, the ways of my former life hung on me like loose skin. Even though women had rights in the new world, I kept thinking about how I had barely escaped that other life, the one where no one would educate me, where anyone could get me pregnant without care. I remember standing in front of the mirror, in 1989, fourteen years old, at my mother's house, trying to see the real me—but there was just a shell of a girl I didn't even know looking back. I felt relief that I was still in my youthful, beautifully perfect adolescent body, that I was in a place where I now had rights. Still, that didn't erase my fears. I made a wish to the Universe that day; I wished to never have children.

Looking back, I recognize that I was a scared little girl—a child—looking at herself in the mirror and creating fantasies. I had taken all my fears with me into this new place.

When I became an adult, I followed that desire. I never wanted to bring a child into this world. I had thought fondly about adopting if the time and resources were ever to present themselves. It is only now, in my later years, that I understand my decision not to have children was much, much deeper than my fear of impregnation. I went through life without unconditional love and support. My brother had the same experience and, ultimately, lost his life because of it. I refuse to take procreation for granted. I know I would love a child unconditionally as I do everyone in my life and every creature on this earth. But, the responsibility of being a mom is too great for my heart to manage.

The cult did that.

Chapter

25

BACK IN OREGON IN THE fall of 2001, I got a call pertaining to my brother. If you recall, the last time I had seen him he bought me a vegan burrito and told me to stop hurting myself. Then, he vanished. Three years later, my father's voice was on the other end of the phone, telling me Michael was free. Somehow, I had already known. I felt his soul existing on the other side; it had been with me for some weeks.

He died of meningitis. He may have just thought he had a cold and downplayed his symptoms. Regardless, I doubt going to a hospital was an option he would've considered. And so, he died, likely alone, not even thirty.

In 2015, in an effort to honor his life, I went to visit my sister on Christmas. In fourteen years, we had never done a ritual for my brother. Not a funeral. Not a commemoration. Nothing. I grieved for him. I felt guilty as hell for not being a better sister. For not protecting him. For not showing him enough love.

My sister and I both insisted on a ritual. Even if it was just the two of us. We lit a candle after everyone went to bed. We focused on three things we loved about Michael. Good memories. Then, we wished him something wonderful for his journey into the afterlife.

Imagine the suffering she and I went through those fourteen years, mourning him without sending his spirit off into the sky with peace. It felt so low, like bad karma.

I returned home to Portland after the holidays. The following Sunday, my partner and I went to church. It was the Sunday after David Bowie had died, struggling for eighteen months with cancer. The ministers at my Unitarian Universalist church talked about death. How it comes and goes like the wind. No one knows when it will darken our doorsteps. No one can predict when the Reaper will take our souls across the river of darkness into the sea of light. This beautiful minister spoke about how we should live our lives awakened to that truth. Living each day like it might be our last. Needless to say, I was grateful that I'd made amends with the spirit of my brother.

About a year ago, upon finishing the first draft of this book, I did a full memorial for Michael. I did an eleven-card tarot read and a month-long meditation ritual. I started the ritual on his birthday, during the cycles of the new moon. I presented a box with the tarot read, crystals, and lots of love and incense to the Buddhist temple here in Portland on the sacred day of one their Buddha's memorial. It felt so good to finally do something wonderful and meaningful for my brother.

Chapter

26

AT SOME POINT IN MY life, I started to experience a paradigm shift in consciousness. As I received my formal education, I began to understand what love and light meant to my own heart. I started to accept and face my shadow, and I carved out a new life for myself. And so, my true beginning emerged.

• • •

I read a lot of Zen Buddhist books. They talk about karma and awakening. They talk about the power of choice. We can learn through suffering. We can learn through karma. But, the golden ticket to our own nirvana is that we can transcend. Recognize. Appreciate. Understand. Move on. And let the cycle of self-destruction blow away in the dust of our cremated past. *Fly, Phoenix—Fly!*

Getting to a place of awareness is painful. When I first began this book, I would cry for hours as I wrote it—seeing my own truth was hard. But, now I am learning to embrace my light and understand my shadow. Learning to use my own power of truth to awaken, postpone judgment, let go of my own attachments to outcome, and ride with the flow and spirit of life itself.

We can analyze something. An event in life. A moment in time. We can look at it clearly. Objectively. That is what post-modern Buddhism teaches—that one of the reasons why people suffer is because of their attachments. Setting myself free from these religious, experiential, and material attachments has allowed me to find a sense of balance, my yin and yang. Finding the perfect balance between our own inner light and shadow creates a playground for inner peace and wellbeing.

Many religions, especially patriarchal ones, teach that we are either good or evil. And, they teach us further that if we aren't submissive to this strand of teaching—the cross, the blood, an outside source bringing redemption—we are fatally flawed, crippled from the cradle to the grave.

By understanding and practicing Buddhism, I've been able to detach myself from the concept of good versus evil. I've been able to study the mechanisms that make my soul tick. I've been able to accept that as a human being, I experience light and shadow and it's all okay.

Sometimes the light may blind me. Sometimes, the shadow may darken my horizon. Regardless, I am comprised of both; we all are. So, for me, there is no redemption by blood. There is no sense of retaliation or shame projected onto us by any god. Just as there is no need for retaliation for my experiences as a child. I was a victim of the shadows. But, I was graced with the ability to find and choose the light.

It is because I choose to see myself and humanity this way that I am open to love and forgiveness. I forgive everything that's happened to me—or happened to others because of me—in my past. I know that even the C.O.G. was a group of human beings—animals with a spirit that longed for something greater than what they had. They, too, longed for a way to understand their lights and to face their own shadows. They chose to give away their wills and souls because that's how they believed it needed to be. The leader of this organization had his own inner demons to face. He was only human, just like the rest of us. I believe in my heart that he was trying to help a strange and lost group of people find redemption. Along the way, he got lost in his own shadow. When I look at the organization and Berg in this way, it helps me forgive. My capacity to forgive has not made me naïve or skewed my memories. I have not been brainwashed by Buddhism or the power of forgiveness. When I look deep into the shadow of my soul—especially when I recollect what happened to Davidito, my brother, and me—I know much of the physical, emotional, psychological, sexual, and spiritual abuse was intentional. It was created to make us weak and vulnerable to Berg, and to keep us under the organization's thumb. There was this illusion that we were free to hear from God. But, their real truth lived beyond the illusion of free will, in tactics used by the organization's leaders to keep us submissive. Maybe Berg thought he was doing the right thing. Regardless of his purest intentions, he was driven by animal impulses and desires, by domination and sexual perversion.

It's in those places of deep awareness that I find forgiveness the most difficult. It's in my darkest shadow that I must find my own courage to grow from that pain, to live my life and let the rest burn in the ashes of yesterday's truth—a truth that is no longer mine.

I believe that my father and mother also had good intentions. They both struggled in different ways to find their place in this world. Even though I do not believe in sin, I know that human beings can be misguided. We can tap too much into our inner darkness, and it can be difficult to find our inner light. We can be frightened by our shadows and run into the arms of anything we think will save us—and that salvation is very different for many people. For some, it will prove to be their demise. Or, it will annihilate those they claim to love.

In my eyes, forgiving is showing empathy to those people, ideas, and things that tried to annihilate me. In forgiving, I have found justice for all.

"If your enemy is hungry, give him food to eat; If he is thirsty, give him water to drink. For you shall reap coals of fire upon his head.

In this truth, you will find your reward" (Proverbs 25:21–22).

Even though I'm not a Christian, I respect other religious systems. I believe in tolerance. I believe in acceptance. I honor all paths to the Divine. I also honor atheists, agnostics, and other forms of spirituality because we are all extensions of the Divine. Each of our journeys is unique and precious. Each of us has something to learn from this life.

A connection with the Divine is our birthright. We don't have to do anything but gracefully accept it. Then, that Divine power is ours—working in us, with us, for us. The "Kingdom of God," or the

Divine presence—which I have been calling it—is already within us, we just have to wake it up.

Nichiren Buddhism uses the lotus flower to describe this concept. A lotus grows in the mud. The flower is birthed with the seed, simultaneously awakening from the mud (or shadow) and reaching into the sun. It embraces the mud at night and the sun in the morning. Its power is all around it and yet it comes from within, from its will to desire and thrive from both the shadow and the light. So, for me, the meaning of light and shadow, yin and yang, is simple: it's the gift of the diversity of pain and pleasure.

I tried to write this book two other times and erased each attempt. It was too painful. I was soaked in sadness. Bitterness. Regret. Suffocating in my own pain. The stars had not aligned for me. Now, my soul is healing. This book is facilitating the rest of the healing I need to grow into my next life with no baggage. Just me. Marie. Out of her rusty cage. Out of her shell of fear. Spreading her wings.

Were my life experiences random? Were they just arbitrary events that were wrapped in pain and horror and tied with thin, frail ribbons of pleasure? Or, was the Universe giving me an opportunity to one day tell my story? To rise above?

I have found the answer to my greatest question: Who am I?

I am nature and nurture, the spiritual and the physical, the emotional and the psychological. I am my mind, my soul, and I have become my will.

What will I build with that truth?

What will I do with my newfound freedom?

What will I do with the spark of the Divine that permeates my soul?

What will I do with my eternal flame?

It doesn't matter, because once we see ourselves in the essence of that shadow and once we comprehend what the purpose is for our light, we can transcend into a sense of belonging and to one of contribution.

We are all connected, after all.

Chapter

27

WITH ALL THIS TALK ABOUT will, self-love, self-respect, etc., I do want to make a point about centering myself. During my many years in weekly therapy, I read a couple books about meditation. I decided to give it a try. I got myself a little Buddha statue with a place for a candle in its center. I bought a candle and some incense. I decided to mix what I was reading about the Law of Attraction, and what I'd read in *The Secret*. I bought a notebook to write affirmations in.

I started to meditate. I would first do a lot of chanting, Nam-myoho-renge-kyo, which is typical to Nichiren Buddhism. It means that we connect with the mystic laws of the Universe through sound—connecting with the Lotus Sutra, the seed of Buddhism. There are levels of consciousness we attach ourselves to, like desire or destruction, and there is also a place of nirvana that we can open up to through meditation. It's centered in the Lotus Sutra, and repeating sounds and words, which happens during chanting, can help us discover it, for chanting has healing properties. I love the idea of connecting with the rhythm and movement of the Universe, so that made perfect sense to me. I focused on clearing my mind from the noise of my daily thoughts. Then, I began to write out positive intentions for what I wanted to create in my life. I turned the focus away from the negative storm, placing more emphasis on authentic desire, on joy. Even though I know that it's with my truest will and spirit that I create, there is definitely no connecting with my truest self without connecting with the Divine first.

The complex idea of co-creating is very divergent, something the leaders in my former cult life would never speak of or advocate. It means working with the Divine, collaborating, because we are connected as if by an umbilical cord. Whether we believe we were created as original human beings or we believe in evolution or reincarnation, there is an aspect of connectedness that we experience, that has existed within our consciousness since before birth. We are a part of the creative energy of this world. Just like a flower is born in the spring and dies in the winter, we die and are reborn in consciousness multiple times over a lifetime. Think about when a person marries or has a baby or gets divorced. Or, when a person is born into a certain religion and then chooses to change their belief system. Those are all examples of a paradigm shift in consciousness. I have experienced death and rebirth countless times in this lifespan.

We were birthed with creativity etched in our brains, like a pre-wired condition. That creativity sets us apart right from the beginning. We create sound with our cries. We create movement with our bodies. We create sympathy through the eyes of those who love us. Creative energy is the generator that guides the vehicle we are in. We will become a part of whatever energy we give ourselves to. In other words, we become our own cause and effect.

148

I destroyed my attachment to the C.O.G. because it created the wrong effect in my life; therefore, it was the wrong cause. Those belief systems did not stem from my consciousness or creative energy. I had to burn that old womb that birthed me into that life and create a new life for myself—a rebirth into something that I chose and decided was right for me.

"I was dead and then I became alive again.
I was lost and then I was found" (Luke 15:24).

Because I believe that my creative spirit is always evolving, I imagine many more deaths and rebirths. Since my spirituality is not set in stone, my soul is always open to the transformative power that gives me life and purpose.

That's the power of freedom. It's the acknowledgement that we create and destroy. We choose our fate with every whisper. Every motion of our bodies. Every pipe song we play. Every choice we make. We are evolving, pure, creative energy. We are the seed of the lotus flower, and we are the flower itself. We are death and life. We face the deepest, darkest mud—dirty and obscured, yet we also face the sun—divine and pure, full of life and rejuvenation. We are the rhythms of the sounds of the undulating roots of creation.

Chapter

28

LEARNING TO LOVE MYSELF HAS been the greatest gift that forgiveness has given me. It has allowed me to enjoy the light of my beautiful ego, yet still remain humble enough to see other people's pain. To feel compassion for their journey. It has allowed me to postpone judgment, to free myself of carrying a cross that never belonged to me—one that no one should ever have to carry.

Humility does not mean that you let people walk all over you. It doesn't make you a patsy or a victim. It doesn't mean you deny yourself or your true light of ego. It just means that you can open your mind to see the plight and experiences of other people. People who are misguided. See them with love and understanding. It doesn't mean we have to agree with what they say or do. It just means that we can feel their pain and still rise above it. We don't go down into the ditch with them. If we are strong enough, and they are willing, we can reach down, offer our hand in love, and help them up. We can all rise above our pain if we want to.

I am grateful for my stubborn and self-willed nature. Yet, I am humbled and grateful for the will of the Divine that merges with my own. To gift me with insight, compassion, and a whole new worldview. The Divine fills me with so much joy. All I want to do is spread the love.

Chapter

29

OVER TIME, ALL OF THOSE self-fulfilling prophecies started to fall into the past. A new day began. I rose to be one of the most successful people at my job. My relationships with my friends, family, and significant others grew stronger, healthier. More real. It was a Divine shift in my personal story. My soul began to heal. I was finally ready to forgive.

When I first got back in touch with my father, we would butt heads like crazy. I remember telling him off during many phone calls. At times, he would even hang up on me. I didn't want him to preach at me. I wanted to vent. To give him a piece of my mind. To get revenge for all the abuse and neglect I'd suffered, much of which I attributed to how and where he raised me.

It took many years for him to go through his own transformation. It took me to change and shift my story—to create a new paradigm of forgiveness. I told myself that if anything, I was forgiving him for me. Even though forgiveness in this regard is, and will be, a life-long process, and even though it is so much easier said than done, I know that forgiving and moving on is the only way my soul will ever find peace.

I knew that holding on to all those demons was poisoning me. Rotting me from the inside out. I knew that I needed to give my father a serious piece of my mind, too. That was a part of the healing process. I needed him to know how much he hurt my brother and me. How much I had suffered. I was not like him. No matter how hard he tried to make me think like him, I was different. I longed for him to respect that. To see my point of view. I ached for him to see me. To respect my views and faith just as much as he wanted me to respect his. I felt like everything in my childhood had always been about him. Never about me or my brother. How we felt. What we wanted. As expected, our views on life and spirituality are still very different.

I have come to realize and accept that we will probably never see eye to eye. But, we have enough in common to make our connection feasible. At times, I feel I was born into the wrong Universe with the wrong father and into the wrong situation. It makes me grieve immensely that my father may never see me and respect me for who I am—for the things I believe. I'm too open-minded. I'm into spiritual principles and a lifestyle that much of his religion condemns. We are broken. And there are some things my mind and heart find unforgivable. But, I have been misguided, too. And when I think of Davidito and what his search for revenge did to him, it scares me not to forgive—it scares me to imagine what I might become if I don't. So, despite the pain, I forge ahead.

Deep in the corridors of my heart, I feel sick about how my father treated my brother. His cruel, hard hand is what destroyed him on the inside, what eventually killed him. Even though his physical death was caused by a disease, he'd died a long time before that. Physical, emotional, and sexual abuse killed him. He suffered severe punishment and neglect—things he didn't deserve. His spirit and creative energy were crushed. Instead of beating love into him, love was beaten out of him. That was, in part, my father's doing. My mother played her role in it, too: she was emotionally unavailable and neglectful.

To be fair, I have my own demons with the way I treated my brother. I tried to gain his love and approval, but I only showed him anger, pain, resentment, and rage. Still, it's that undeserved forgiveness that we give, like giving water to our enemy, which gives us a chance to heap coals of fire upon their heads. I hope that they will find their own karma at the end of their road. I hope that we can, through catharsis, discover our own personal transformation. The way to our own acceptance, awakening, and transcendence is through forgiveness.

Finally, after years of healing, my father and I agree to disagree. We have this flowing and respectful relationship because I choose to forgive him, and he forgives me for my anger and rage. (Admittedly, it's still a work in progress, but that is the goal.) I am learning to see through eyes of understanding and empathy. I am not under his thumb anymore. I am my own person.

Now, I can see that he was just a lost hippie in his twenties. He was looking for meaning in his life. This organization was how he found it. My father's father, my grandfather, killed himself in his garage when my father was thirteen—carbon monoxide poisoning. My dad had no real father, either. His father was physically abusive. He used a hard hand and a belt. His parents were emotionally and spiritually neglectful. It's a wonder my father is even alive today.

Understanding that makes it easier for me to forgive him. After all, he had to forgive his own father.

One of my main goals in writing this book is to make an attempt at ending the cycles of abuse and neglect that happen to children in our world. Abuse trickles down from generation to generation. In my training to work at the prison with those teenage boys, I learned that these cycles are hard to break. Most of those kids had been abused and neglected—they were victims that became victimizers.

My father did what he thought was right. As misguided as it was, he was acting based on all he knew. I did the same thing with my mother. I looked at her life in its totality; she did the best she could, too. It's taken me a lot of years to manage my abandonment issues, to work through my struggles with relationships and trust, to empathize with her journey.

Once I decided to forgive my parents, I could see clearly to forgive just about everyone in the world. I began to see the world through the eyes of compassion, mercy, and grace. I was also able to forgive myself for not being a better sister to my brother, and all the other naïve and ignorant things I had done to others and myself. I was able to begin the journey of loving myself. To have the utmost compassion for myself and respect for my own identity.

Chapter

30

FINDING LOVE HAS BEEN A challenge. One of the reasons I've been able to keep an open heart so consistently for so long is because I have found my muse—my ticket to Divine awareness. It's not just meditation, it is music, art, literature, intellectual dialogue, a great career, great relationships, and finding my hidden talent, which is writing.

I encourage you to find your muse, whatever that may be; let it nourish you with the inspiration you need to continue on this difficult road we call life. Find your hidden talent, and no matter what anyone else says, utilize it. In finding my muse and my talents, I have accessed my powerful soul. And now I can share it.

"Don't cast your pearls before swine, lest they trample them under their feet, turn again and rend you" (Matthew 7:6).

I agree wholeheartedly. Don't give anything of yourself away to anyone or any charismatic leader, ideology, political view, or religious conceptualization, unless you see fit. I have taken my power back, and so can you.

I laugh now when I think of my childhood indoctrination. Education was always forbidden. The world was a spawn of Satan and the information highway was a road to destruction. How silly. Did they really think I would be played a fool forever?

If we shelter ourselves from our truth, how can we ever be part of the real dynamic of the Universe? The journey of being human?

In that truth lies my purpose.

Chapter

31

I AM NO LONGER THAT fourteen-year-old girl at the foot of a world I did not know how to live in, scared and scarred, underneath that tree with my brown bag and my overdone makeup, wondering how I could fit in a place that was so big and so completely beyond my control.

I have learned by my own experiences that I have an amazing desire for freedom. I have a determination to live a life of my choosing. If anyone puts me in a box, I will rebel. But, if I feel the inspiration of the fire of life, I will rise above the darkness within me until I am whole and complete.

There have been places in my mind where I get stuck. There are places where I still experience post-traumatic stress. My mind sometimes gets fixated on things that are not helpful to my transcendence. The key is to remember who we truly are. I have to remember who I AM. My true self. My higher self. My own eternal flame. My personal divine energy and power. A power that no one can take away from me. Not today. Not tomorrow. Not ever. Because that power in me is mine, and it is untouchable.

Chapter

32

WE ALL HAVE A KILLER and a healer inside. We all have the potential to be racist, discriminatory, arrogant, controlling. We can choose to be loving, kind, self-aware, and part of the co-creative nature of life. We are a perfect concoction of light and shadow. But, the most important and beautiful thing is we have the power to choose awareness in order to manifest the outcomes we truly seek.

I believe we are searching for that perfect understanding. What each of us wants more than anything is to be understood. To be valued. To be respected. To see beyond the darkness in each other's eyes, into the transparent, intoxicating beauty.

But, I believe as soon as we surrender our will to another, we lose ourselves. It is only within the Divine that we can release our fears and our worries and become enraptured in the co-creative energy that allows us to foster more prosperous outcomes for our lives.

These are some ideas that I welcomed, just to break free from so much abyss and darkness inside my soul. All the while, the answers were right in my heart. The truth was in me, my truth. I was a manifestation of the Divine in human form. The Universe was already here, I just had to wake it up inside.

Chapter

33

TO THIS DAY, I OFTEN sit with a glass of wine, listening to music and weeping for Davidito, my brother, and myself. What helps me get through it is a book called *Healing Grief: Reclaiming Life After Any Loss* by James Van Praagh. It talks about the importance of grieving and the healing powers it provides. I don't think Davidito knew how to grieve. I doubt he had anyone's arms to go to, no family. I doubt he ever knew his biological father. He never had anyone to help him find his purpose or a life outside the organization. He couldn't handle the world. He didn't have any tools to figure out how to learn to be alive. He shut off his emotions, repressed his humanity, and became a suicidal killer. That's what stealing his free will did to him.

As I think about Davidito and the short-lived revenge he sought on his nanny, I recognize that moment cost him his life and any chance he had of finding his true, authentic self.

There is no way on earth I should still be alive today, much less be an educated woman and in my right mind. My family even wrote me off as dead to the world. I know now that I had guardians watching over me. I know in my heart that everything happens for a reason. I believe that my purpose in living through such craziness was to write this book so that others facing similar situations can use the opportunity to find their voices—to express themselves in an unadulterated way, without shame or guilt. Their lives have meaning. They can live with purpose. No matter what anyone has been through, no matter how harmful and terrifying, good can come from it.

C h a p t e r

34

WHEN I WAS AT PORTLAND State University, before I transferred to a private Christian college, I studied a lot of liberal subjects. In one of my classes, the professor discussed something he termed the panoramic theory.

The principle behind this theory reminded me of the natural process of apoptosis and of the brainwashing I'd received as a child. A prison was used as the setting to test this theory. In the center of this prison was a huge tower, encircled with windows. From each window, there was a jail lord with a gun pointing downward on the open area where the prisoners were released daily. Soon enough, the prisoners were so conditioned to expect those guns, expect death should they misbehave, that not only were the guns unnecessary, the jail lords didn't even need to be there. Fear had been established. The prisoners had been trained.

I love this story because it reminds me of how, in general, we are all conditioned to behave. At work, on the roads, in school.... It's like we wouldn't know how to live a balanced life and respect others and their rights if we didn't have "guns" pointing at our heads. I recognize that this may be part of our current human condition. We are still that primitive in our thinking. I believe the whole reason we cling so desperately to fear as a motivator is because we are conditioned to believe that fear is the tool that will keep us in line. Personally, I feel fear is a lazy tool passed on to us from the evolutionary states of consciousness from which we were bred.

I understand that fear is one of our best societal motivators, but we abuse it. We know that if we scare a person, society, or country, they will believe like we do and follow what we deem correct.

But, what if those controls were to slip through the cracks? What difference does it make if we scare someone into a belief system that is not their own? It doesn't make any difference because once those fear tactics are no longer in place, reversion will ultimately occur. Or worse, a hollow feeling of total aloneness; a state of confusion; a state of deep sorrow; a psychotic break, like in the case of Davidito—these are the things that will happen.

The organization I grew up in wanted to create change in the world, but their methodologies became traps. They motived through control and fear. It wasn't that all their euphoric ideas about an idealistic society were all wrong. It's that the leader, or leaders, felt that the only way to get people to follow suit was through fear tactics, manipulation, and control. And they rolled in sexual abuse on top of everything else. The guns were no longer pointed at our heads after a time, but the fear of betrayal was ever-present.

Like with my father, I didn't need any more spankings after a while. The indoctrination and conditioning became enough to keep me in line. Until I left the cult and moved into the real world.

The truth is: I stayed in line to avoid the spanking. It wasn't that I believed, I feared retribution.

Did the prisoners in the panoramic theory study suddenly become well-mannered? Or did they, too, fear the punishment?

Chapter

35

WHAT IS LOVE? I THOUGHT giving my body to another was love. I thought if I sacrificed that precious, physical piece of me, regardless of how I felt, I was gaining approval, acceptance, and receiving love in return. Remember, I was taught that self-sacrifice and self-denial was the only mode of operation, the code of ethics, and a form of love that I had to live by to be accepted and considered holy. This was strung throughout all of my religious indoctrination. After all, the Bible says that we should deny ourselves and take up our cross and follow whatever this guy or that guy or this leader or that charismatic prophet or that parent says to do. It leaked into my life like poison.

• • •

Recently, I spoke to a coworker about this (she was not affiliated with my childhood organization). She said she had been date raped when she was nineteen. She expressed how she's still dealing with the post-traumatic stress in her thirties. All of the sexual encounters I had, some of which would be considered statutory rape, I consented to. I was never violently forced to do anything. Regardless, I know now that I was digging deep for love. I wanted it so badly. I needed it like a drug. I may have felt moments of something I considered to be love, and I did finally end up with a couple boyfriends that were not just flings or one-night stands. I thought that I might give them a chance at loving me, and I tried to love them. But, I was never ready. Love flew by like a mythological creature in a dream, taunting me.

I don't regret all of my sexual experiences, especially as I got older and had more control—when I knew myself better. But, I would not have given my body to so many of those men or women had I'd known and loved myself like I do now. I was never technically raped, no, but I was sexually abused by pedophiles as a child, and drugged and drunk during statutory rape as a teenager, among other abuses (like at the hands of that one pervert, who tied me up to teach me "acting techniques" when I was sixteen). I can reason beyond those experiences now, but I am still affected by them through my subconscious, in my memories.

So, what is love to me now? I think I'm still discovering it....

The Universe speaks to me through everything. I saw a bumper sticker the other day that read: *The dead do not tell tales.* That was the Universe speaking to me. What good is my life? What good are my talents and holy gifts? What good are the stories that I have to tell? What good is my book, *The Gift of Will*, if I cannot tell the tale while I'm here? I'm dedicated to the fact that everything I've experienced in my life has been, and is, for a reason.

170

Christ might've been one of the first human rights activists of his time. "Do unto others as you would have them do unto you." Simple, right? Don't violate my human rights, and I won't violate yours.

Believe me, amidst the horrors that I remember of my childhood, I do take away some silver linings. My favorite Bible story was of the woman who was a "sinner." She had fallen into her own passion with another man who was not her husband. Who knows why. Maybe her husband was an asshole. Maybe her husband was abusive. Maybe he forced himself on her when she wasn't in the mood. Maybe he didn't show her enough love and respect. Who knows? The point of the story is that she gave herself to another. She let her passion and desire take her heart. She was going to be stoned to death by the religious culture of her day because of it. This Christ figure sat, waiting for the stoning. As the story goes, he wrote something in the dirt on the ground. Maybe he was just doodling, contemplating how he would save this poor woman's life. Maybe he thought she was beautiful or regarded her as a human being with rights to love who she chose.

When those who judged her came to stone her to death, they asked for this strange man's opinion. Should they kill or not kill this woman? Christ said that if anyone were without fault or sin, they should be the one to kill her. Cast the first stone.

Christ was acting as a human rights advocate, fighting for others. This eventually killed him.

Chapter

36

I READ ABOUT THE LAW of Attraction and the Power of Intention. I have seen my own intentions, words, thoughts, actions, and choices mark and pave the way for serious manifestation. My life is a canvas. I am painting my creations by speaking my truth as the picture unfolds. Then, my world, and how I see it, comes to life for others to enjoy and study.

My personal experiences have helped me to recognize the dangers of blanket categorization. I have learned to question absolutely everything. I ask questions like: What are my rights? Who is my dignified self? What does my spiritual, emotional, and intellectual self want and need?

In that awareness, I find a pathway of self-discovery. I never arrive at one set of conclusions. I am transforming throughout each facet of my life, gaining more understanding. With that understanding comes compassion, for myself and others. It allows me to separate myself from other people's opinions of what's right for me. It allows me to see my animal and spirit self, evolving, interconnected with my heart and soul—as a permanent extension of the Divine.

The self-respect I possess now has allowed me to create boundaries that are important in my own personal evolution with the Divine.

I love this quote by Oscar Wild: *"The aim of life is self-development. To realize one's nature perfectly—that is what each of us is here for."*

My life is about living that truth every day and not settling for anything less.

Chapter

37

BECAUSE MY BROTHER AND I were forced to read the Bible as children, I *actually* read it. It was our punishment—a way for us to think through the errors of our ways and be consumed with an indoctrination that was supposed to enlighten us and set us free. We were forced to memorize it, too, and I don't mean like a churchgoer can recite Sunday service without thinking. I would sit in the corner of a room when I was being disciplined and I would have to memorize certain chapters and then recite them and discuss the message intensely. I suppose I was a bad girl often, because I have the Bible memorized backwards and forwards.

There are many beautiful stories that focus on humanity struggling to evolve and coming to a place of higher consciousness. To connect with the Divine. To connect with the Lord. To overcome difficulty. To love and find mercy and strength in the face of the hardship. It's also a violent, bloody book. It's a book about revenge and war. It's a book about people begging and pleading with God to absolve and protect them. It's a book I've rarely seen anyone talk about, not for real.

I remember sitting in the corner of a room, begging God to forgive me for the errors of my ways and to get me out of the damn corner and back into the approving wings of my father. I remember reading about these stories, wondering how we were all about peace when so much bloodshed and war was sanctioned by the god of this book. There was so much punishment, isolation, shame, fear, and death—it made my heart quiver. I felt so overwhelmed, but I kept my thoughts and my heart to myself.

The Bible says that rebellion is as the sin of witchcraft, and stubbornness is as iniquity and idolatry (1 Samuel 15:23). This damns me right from the start because I am both stubborn and rebellious, among the other Pagan rituals I practice A renowned woman, Barbara Marx Hubbard, began to think differently in the 1970s about the world and about the human species. She writes in her book, *The Hunger of Eve,* that "*…In our age we'll evolve either toward the consciousness of oneness and transcendence, or to some form of death—whether by fire or ice.*" She goes on to explain, "*We're really confronted with an unprecedented pragmatic situation: the tools for Armageddon or transformation.*" She speaks my truth completely.

I will resist anything that does not feel right to me, no matter what any book says. I used to find myself with lingering thoughts: *Am I evil and rebellious for wanting to be so free?*

I find myself recalling the moments in my life where fear made me crawl back into my cage.

The big explosion of Mother Nature that birthed me into the world did it for a good reason. She knew that my journey would be tough, and that I would have to endure many scars in order to find peace of mind. But she knew I was worth it.

Finding my own inner truth and freedom is well worth the struggle it has taken me to get to where I am today; it's worth the struggles that I will face in the future to continue to find my authentic self and my own path to awareness, redemption, and transcendence.

I am an eclectic believer. No rule book or dictatorial perception can tell me where my roots have come from. I will always choose to be free: knowledge is my greatest gift, along with my will, my heart, and my soul.

The gift of life and will is not to be toyed with. Life is not a test. For me, co creation with the Divine, whether I am heathen, a saint, both or none, is the only way to create the most powerful energy of the Universe—true love.

Chapter

38

WHEN MY FATHER AND I reconnected, he reminded me to find my purpose. I now understand what finding my purpose means. Being a voice is my purpose. It's my mission and destiny. I want to empower others. I want others to be proud of who they are. To find their holy gifts. To actualize their purpose. To speak their truth. To find their muses. To live by their own destiny.

We should all tell our stories. We can find our purpose in our raw energy and in our true identities and souls. We can rise beyond survival. We can forgive. We can thrive. We can fight the victimization of what humans do to other humans in the name of control, power, and fear. We can be connected with our true selves and the Divine.

What does it mean to create our own worlds? We're often taught that we shouldn't want anything—we should just be grateful for what we have. I'm going to propose something very simple: If we don't want, we can't create. If we don't create, we have nothing.

There's a Post-it note that I keep on my desk at work. It reads: *Create something that will live forever.* We get one shot at this life. We don't know for certain what it means to cross over to the other side. But, we do know from history that people can create things that will live forever in the hearts and minds of those they leave behind.

There is a scripture where Christ is talking about the people that criticized him. He said that his critics were clean on the outside, but inside they were full of dead men's bones and corruption (Matthew 23:27). During my research into goddess theology, I think about what it means to be clean. It's like the idea of cracking the code to the meaning of life. Being clean is to feel bold enough to speak our truths, our hearts, and embrace ourselves fearlessly while not being afraid of the opinions of the rest of the world.

At times, I do hate. I ask myself, *When will pure love dissolve my hatred and win?* I hope and believe that through love and understanding I can dissolve my hatred into awareness, transcendence, and an opportunity to experience the bliss, wonder, exhilaration, and limitlessness of life.

Energy never dies. I want my energy to be that of the energy of love, now and forever. Writing my story helps. It is therapeutically perfect. I urge every human being to write their story. If Judgment Day is anything, it's only us, human beings, telling our stories to the Universe and hoping to be understood.

I will always carry my scars, just like David Jones Bowie carried his beautiful scars to the grave and beyond. Just like so many other beautiful artists, musicians, writers, and creative people have. We can make music out of our misery and sing our songs to the Universe.

The opinion I have of myself and my perception of the world is the most important opinion I can have. Others will influence my perception, when, and if, I let them. But, it is up to me to choose how I will see the world, what perspectives I take in, and which ones I leave behind. I do what feeds me—nothing more, nothing less. It feeds me to believe in humanity. It feeds me to love myself. It feeds me to bring food and water to countries that are dying of starvation and thirst. It feeds me to help children. It feeds me to write. It feeds me to be creative and to admire others' creativity. It feeds me to be in love with music, the world, my feelings. It feeds me to tell my story. It feeds me to remember that I'm alive. It feeds me to live. It feeds me to be passionate. It feeds me to be an influence in this beautiful world. It feeds me to always ask why, and to never take anything for granted. These are the elements that form the truths of my reality, my perceptions, my choices, and my life.

The power, ultimately, is in my hands. What will I do with my power?

• • •

I am proud to say that today I have a beautiful relationship with my mother and father—though distant. I have worked diligently to ensure that truth would be mine. My parents have both worked at it in their own way, as well. It has been one of my life's purposes—after ten-plus years of therapy and life coaching—to say that I honor my family unconditionally: no shame, no blame, and no guilt to hang over their heads in my name, or in the name of my brother. At least, I try. (Make no mistake it's easier said than done, but it's the ultimate goal.)

I have learned a few very important ideas from my mother, who has been on her own spiritual journey for many years now. She always tells me that we create our own reality and that cooperating components of the Universe are always working on our behalf. She lives her life by that code, and it truly works magic. She has evolved in wonderful ways. She is kind and insightful, and I am always glad when we have the opportunity to connect. She is an independent but spiritual creature. I'm certain I got my tenacious and resilient spirit from her.

My father is still very much devoted to his Bible, but he does his best to listen to me (when he can muster the courage to do so) and accept that his daughter is a divergent believer on a completely different wavelength. He's also given me good, fatherly advice, which has helped me make it through challenging times in the real world. I honor him for that.

I feel connected with my brother, who is on the other side in another plane of consciousness. Sometimes, I think I sense the energy of Davidito somewhere in that mix, as well.

My younger sister and I are the best of friends. We chat and hang out all the time. The greatest gift, for me, is that my sister does not harbor any resentment toward me for the attitudes I held or the actions I took as a teenager. She doesn't feel that I ruined her life in any way. She is open-hearted and an amazing, grounded, and personable human being. I am honored to call her a sister and friend.

My half-sister is in my life, too, and she is amazing, graceful, and a wonderful person. I am honored that forgiveness has brought me these gifts.

I found the most angelic editor in the Universe. Her help and support in writing this book is a magical gift. She is one of my guardian angels in this material world, and I could not have completed this project without her. With her help, I am writing a book of poetry, a book of dreams, young adult fiction fantasy books, and possibly children's books, which are my passion.

Even though reality is beyond our total control, and events will happen that we cannot change, what we can control is how we perceive those events, how we manage our perceptions, and how we construct our reality in the face of those truths.

Even though I have forgiven the sources of all the confusing brainwashing I experienced, and I have forgiven the people in my life that provoked my mental and emotional breakdown, I still have the right as a human being to not adopt their beliefs. My psyche, my mind, my heart, my soul, and what I let into the sacred temple of my body is my choice.

Forgiving doesn't mean I want them in my psyche, it just means I have stepped into awareness and made peace with the storms that struck my life. I have had to forgive myself for the storms I caused and for my ignorance, even though I recognize the patterns that were created in my consciousness through nature and nurture. I forgive for myself and accept that I cannot control what happened in my past. All I can do is move forward one step at a time, to create a new world, which is my future, and to make my world and my life a better place today.

That is the focus of this book. We are given our experiences, but once we walk with an open heart into awareness, we can create a better reality for ourselves despite our past and mistakes. We can find peace and balance within the yin/yang of our lives to create more of what we want, and we can have the courage to flush out what we don't. Awareness can help us deal with our pain, our pleasure, and define our own light and shadow.

Finally, I am, and will always be, a daughter of our Mother Earth. I will always be her child. I am like the wind, the sea, and the stars. I will never be anything that can be controlled, but I will surrender to the co-creative energy when it appears right to do so—so I can discover my highest potential and let old paradigms of thinking go.

In my heart, I will always be a wildfire that grows and flies as she sees fit. I will let Mother Earth continue to baptize me with her wonder, awe, and splendor. I will always be her daughter, just as I am the goddess-like stars in the gleaming sky.

Peace be with you.
Blessed Be.
Believer Be.
Keep calm and carry on.

Sincerely,
Marie

FINAL NOTE

Ever since I opened up about writing this book, so many resources have come my way, reminding of a purpose that's greater than me.

People in my circle of influence send me books that were written by courageous people who have undergone similar abuse. My aunt, for example, sent me a book by David Carr, *American Trauma: America's Silent War on Children.* Carr's book mirrors mine in so many ways, I've wondered—*are we reading each other's minds?*

I realize he is not reading my mind, and I am not reading his. The truth is, these cycles of abuse create the same destructive paradigm for all abused children. In his book, David Carr talks about Erin Runnion, my cousin. Her daughter, Samantha Runnion, was kidnapped, sexually assaulted, and murdered. He talks about Erin's amazing journey as a mother, going through incredible and inexplicable pain.

David was molested by men when he was a child. As I read his book, I couldn't help but cry, thinking about my brother. David reminded me so much of him. But, he, like me, wants to create a platform where the world can benefit from these tragedies—by bringing awareness where others would use fear and shame to keep us silent.

David writes in his book, "*What's great about breaking the cycle is, once you start to do it, the shades on your canvas start to change.*" His words are true. Once you choose awareness over ignorance, the Universe will give you exactly what you ask for—the ability to help others to become aware as well.

My cousin Erin is writing a book, too, about the daughter she lost. I suppose it runs in my family. She has not buried her head in the sand. Instead, Erin created a foundation called The Joyful Child. She educates parents and anyone who will listen on how to recognize predators and prevent abuse and neglect. She is a shining star and a soul worth listening to.

All of us who write books like this one want the world to understand one thing—abuse is real, and we all need to have a voice. Together, as one, we can stop the cycles of abuse, learn to love each other, and empower, protect, and educate our children.

I am including a list of books that have helped me in my healing process. It's a long list, but leaders are readers and I want to open the minds of my readers to expand their perception of reality. I challenge my readers to open their minds and expose themselves to ideas that, as divergent as they may be, might be the catalyst needed to create change.

My underlying theme is a warning to those who might attempt to start an organization like the one I came from; or, for those who might be considering joining such an organization:

My light is stronger than your darkness.

I am reminded of other organizations that also dragged their converts down a fast-track to destruction. Groups such as the Branch Davidians, whose leader sacrificed all the members of his congregation, women and children included, in order to preserve his own image: they all ended up dying for David Koresh's personal vision. Jim Jones's group: he poisoned the weak and the helpless with his lies and deceit. His venom ended up costing all of his members—men, women, and children—their lives. They gave their wills to him, and he destroyed them.

I want to bring awareness to all organizations, secular or religious. Children have rights. They should be able to choose for themselves what their paths will be. Our greatest job as parents or role models is to help them do just that.

Be aware. All that glitters is not gold. Choose wisely. Be a voice for the oppressed and abused. Be true to yourself and never take giving your will away lightly. Yours is the gift of will. May you create an amazing reality with it.

I dedicate this book to my brother, Michael, to Davidito, and to all the other second-generation adults that left that organization. You are not alone. You don't have to go through what we went through to be whole and beautiful. You have a right to live your life as you choose, and nothing can take that gift away from you. This book is also for all the others who have suffered from religious abuse or oppression or any other type of abuse.

We fight together, all over the world, to silence the voice of abuse and replace it with the voice of strength. Remember Malala Yousafzai, the little girl who spoke out for the rights of children to obtain an education: she nearly died, shot by a terrorist because she fought for the rights of young girls to go to school. Remember girls like the one who got shot for choosing love over being forced to marry an older man when she was still a child. She survived and will live to remind us of the abuses we justify by religion, politics, culture, etc. (Watch the documentary: *A Girl in the River*.) Let us rise above the abuse. The promise of truth will shine brighter than any darkness.

The ironic thing is that I feel my brother's presence with me more now that I am writing this book than I have in years. I feel that he is watching me, caring for me, helping me, and speaking his truth, too—our truth. He reminds me that we are not alone. There are many of us, and we have a voice. We will not be silenced.

Finally, remember who you are. Find your inner I AM. Be the divine creature you are. Never give up on your goals and dreams. And remember, you can create the life you choose. No one has that power more than you do. Be true to you!

I love you all so much.

I am not your rolling wheels, I am the highway.
I am not your carpet ride, I am the sky.

—*Chris Cornell*

ABOUT THE COVER

The Universe and I have created *familiars*. They are my guardians. They protect my imagination. They give me solace. They comfort me. They are magnificent and pure.

My first familiar is a black dragon. She has rainbow wings and I call her Phoenix because the legend of the Phoenix reminds me of rising above the ashes of defeat and death. I also have a Mage, who is pure light. The strength of his light keeps me grounded. I have Twinkilu and Twinkila. They are my dual energy fairies. I have my snake. She is purple and green. Her name is Mystery because my life has been such a mystery to me. I have a golden leaf, which represents prosperity. And I have a lotus flower, which resembles the goddess of purity: sleeping in the mud but rising into the sun. It's impossible to fully explain or express exactly how my familiars support me—the best way I can describe it is that they take me to an alternative reality.

When I decided to write this book in 2013, I was in my bedroom, going to sleep. I was lost in my imagination. There, in that space of vacant thought, I imagined my inner warrior rising up to fight on my behalf.

Suddenly, I thought of a dragon. She was black and furious. Her energy was warm and welcoming. I heard a voice in my mind that said, "What will you do with her?" I said, "I will call her Phoenix. I will give her the wings of the rainbow. That way, she will always fight for us. She will fight for diversity. For the divergent. For my life."

Soon, I began to play with Phoenix. She would listen to my voice. She would react to my soul. She was a living, breathing, piece of me—a part of my essence. She gave me power to create with her. To send my soul into flight using her as my platform. I felt the darkness around her overcome me.

Then, I saw the most amazing light. That light was Mage. He was so powerful and sturdy. He did not waver. He did not refuse my power. He let me penetrate him as he penetrated my being. I saw his staff was light. It hit the ground around me with an unimaginable fury. He called to me to name him. But, I could call him nothing more. He was Mage. He would be my pillar of protective light.

I knew that these were my familiars. I felt them close to me, calling me to use them. To use my power through them to fight and ward off the weaknesses that compelled me to beg, to crawl, and to back down from writing this book.

It wasn't too long after that I felt something strange in my womb. It was night again. I was lying in my bed, feeling the loss of not having children, remembering my love for the cycles of life. There, in that moment of recognition, I saw her. No, I felt her. She was crawling inside my womb. I closed my eyes and there she was. A vision of perfection. She was a green snake with a ribbon of purple woven into the skin on her slim body. Her face was large. She looked straight into my eyes. She had very small wings; they fluttered with her innocence. She demonstrated her fierceness. Her power. She turned toward my Phoenix and the light of Mage to become one with them. Her face drew inward with wild aspiration. She looked at me and the fierceness of her eyes had changed. She was no longer a docile pet. She was extreme. She was vicious. She would fight for me. She would be my inner strength. She would happily devour my worst of enemies—even the enemies of my mind.

I felt torn. There was this connection I'd made with my passion for reptiles like the snake. But, my heart was wounded from the mythological stories that we tell. I knew this, and so I called her Mystery because she was my anomaly of self. She was that mystical being inside, reminding me that I was perfect and to never bow down to the unwanted projections of others. She would give me comfort. She surrounded me with her skin and her sleekness, warming me in the most perfect way. She was me, and I was her.

When my final familiar came to me, I felt that two worlds were being created in my mind. One was pure and innocent of the dangerous myths we tell ourselves are our truths. The other was the raw and cruel mind of the demon that fed on my insecurities.

I wondered if I deserved them—these familiars. My final familiar looked at me. She was a fairy with wild hair and large, pale eyes. She turned with my angst and my fear and twirled around, fast as lightning. I saw her destroy all my fears. She reminded me that we are always duel in our essence. We are vicious yet pure. One side of my energy was cleansed by the purity of the other. She became my fiercest warrior. She slays unwanted thoughts and insecurities that would otherwise plague my psyche and affect my life in a negative way.

This is how my familiars were formed. We give each other power. We will never be apart. When I feel alone or isolated, I see myself with the horns of a Pagan goddess. I stand with the power of my familiars on a sea of fire. I raise the staff of my Mage. I send my fairies into the dark with the power of lightning. I rest in the passion of Mystery as she rests in my belly. My womb of creation. I ride my dragon off into the dark sky as we head for the full moon.

ACKNOWLEDGMENTS

I want to thank a few people that have helped me along the road to finding my true self and my gift of will. Thank you, Char (my first therapist by my own choosing), for listening to me and being so clinical that you allowed me to look at my life objectively for the first time—without shame, fear, or guilt.

Thank you, Melissa McMurray, my therapist and life coach. You understand me because you grew up Mormon and can relate on a spiritual level to my scars.

Thank you to my teachers, in college and in life, for helping me to recognize my own potential and for helping me to believe I could be a better me.

Thank you to my amazing friends, who are my new family now, for your undying support, postponed judgment, and the love and admiration you've maintained through every bit of this challenging writing process.

Thank you to my beautiful sister for loving me unconditionally, for never resenting me even though I was a wrecking ball in your life, and for choosing to be not only a sister but one of my best friends in the entire Universe.

Thank you to my partner for your undying and unconditional love, and for putting up with me when I can't stop crying over things you can only imagine but can faintly understand.

Thank you to my spiritual guides, my guardians, and my familiars who protect me and reassure me.

Thank you to my mother and father, who have dealt with this difficult process even though it has been painful for you, too. I thank you for your unconditional support, and for being willing to try to build something new and fresh from the past—that is my true desire.

Thank you to all of the spiritual forces of the Universe in human form that have helped to build me into the woman that I am.

Thank you, Science of Mind, Unitarian Universalist, Buddhist, Hindus, and all of the spiritual forces that have helped me to pursue a spirituality that is authentic and original and true to who I am without the projections of others.

Thank you to my dear Messianic Jewish friends for your unconditional benevolence, compassion, kindness, and love. You are my family now, too.

Thank you to Cooperating Components of the Universe that work on our behalf. Universe: you blow me away with so much love and support.

Thank you to my beautiful, amazing, and wonderful brother, Michael, for inspiring me to write and for reaching out from the other side and working with me through every single word and step of creating this book. You are my hero and my muse. I love you.

Thank you to all the people who read this book. Whatever you have been through, you are my heroes. I hope you will find peace in your hearts, too, with your past and with who you are. May you tell your stories and open your heart to the Universe and watch Her take you under her wing, understanding everything.

Last, but certainly not least, thank you to my editor and friend, Lisa Marie Cerasoli. Thank you for seeing what laid behind the veil of my mind, for seeing value in my story, and for giving without expecting to receive anything in return—like a fountain of love and light. You remind me that there are people out there that can see right through the façade and come out with a new paradigm of consciousness. You are pure light and love in my eyes.

I love you all.
Namaste.

Deep thanks to the authors who have motivated me to thrive. These are just a few. There are so many more:

Tama Keives
Depak Chopra
Rumi
Mike Dooley
Daisaku Ikeda
Lotus Sutra—Ikeda version
Marcus Borg—*Jesus and Buddha*
Carol Christ
Shari Arison
Mary Pat Fisher
Stuart Perrin
Ernest Holms—*Science of Mind*
Eldan Taylor
Anthony Robbins
Abraham and Esther Hicks—*Law of Attraction*
The Secret
Dr. Wayne Dyer
Michael J. Gelb
Barbara Marx Hubbard
Tarot
James Van Praagh
Anita Diamant—*The Red Tent*
Michael Bernard Beckwith
John Eldridge
Carl Jung—Liber Novus—*The Red Book*
Pronoia—Brezsny
Tara Prach
Santos Bonacci

THE GIFT *of* WILL

www.ingramcontent.com/pod-product-compliance
Lightning Source LLC
Chambersburg PA
CBHW072344090426
42741CB00012B/2921